Age in Good Time

Lives and Lessons from Seven Men in their Seventies

(or how to lead a good life)

By

Larry Matthews

W & B Publishers

USA

W & B Publishers

For information:
W & B Publishers
9001 Ridge Hill Street
Kernersville, NC 27284

www.a-argusbooks.com

ISBN: 9781942981947

Book Cover designed by Dubya

Printed in the United States of America

Age in Good Time

Table of contents

Page #

Author's note to readers

This book is about seven men who have led successful lives and are now in their eighth decade. A couple of them will have moved into their ninth by now. They all have something to say. It is not an exaggeration to say that every one of them has lived the American Dream. They began humbly and, as boys and young men, faced heavy odds that they would go far in life, much less as far as they have.

This is a book of stories, a compendium of experiences and lessons. Picture seven men gathered around a large table, talking about where they were and how they got to where they are.

You will read about a scientist, a cop, two famous broadcasters, two military officers and a spy. At times it will lift you up and at other times it will break your heart.

I want to thank every one of them for sharing their stories, good, bad and heartbreaking. There are lessons here for anyone who looks at old men and assumes there's nothing left.

Old In Good Time

Lives and Lessons from Seven Men in their Seventies

(or how to lead a good life/)

By Larry Matthews

Wisdom is with aged men, With long life is understanding.

Job 12:12

or

Old age and the passage of time teach all things.

Sophocles

Introduction

In 1776 a man born into what would become the United States of America could expect to live to the ripe old age of thirty-five. Half the population of white males was under eighteen. Surviving childhood was an accomplishment. Disease, accidents, violence and the general miseries of living in a primitive state took their toll. Old age was rare and often limited to the privileged, who ate better, lived better and generally had more comfortable lives. During the nineteenth century America's *average* age was around eighteen. It's in the mid-thirties today. The rise is due to the increase in the number of old people.

Americans' lifespans had crept up to forty-five by 1900 and today is in the high seventies for men and low eighties for women, a life span that was all but unheard of a few centuries ago. Old age was once seen as unnatural, a freak accident of nature. The human body, it was thought, was not designed for a long life. Work hard, breed, and die.

There are about forty-million people over the age of sixty in the United States today. That number is expected to double by 2050. By 2030 one out of five of us will be over sixty. It's the same in other advanced countries.

Young people, myself included at one time, don't really see old people. They may listen to a story now and then but for the young, white hair and sagging skin are not on the radar. We're "the old guy" who walks his dog or shops at Safeway in the afternoon. We feel the sunshine on a warm day and it may trigger memories of afternoons long ago with girls in summer dresses. Or we may just want to take a nap.

In this book you will look into the lives of seven men in their seventies. All of them accomplished, some astoundingly so. You will hear from men who have achieved great things. You will hear from ordinary guys like me. All of the men in this book will share with you the things they have learned about life and the lessons they have learned about themselves. We all have regrets. We all have things we are proud of. We have all suffered loss. We have loved and been loved. We have one important advantage over the young. We have been where they are. They have not been where we are. With luck, one day they will be.

This is not my story, although I am a septuagenarian and grew up in the same world that will be described by these men. My role is a kind of moderator. I interviewed these men over many months to present their stories, their lives. Here and there I will offer an opinion or a judgement, thereby removing myself from any role that could be described as "journalist." I was one for many years but here I am merely a storyteller.

The stories will begin in childhood and move through teenage years and into adulthood, marriage, divorce, illness, careers, more marriages, middle age, and eventually to retirement. These are very personal stories. If you are young, pay attention. Getting to old age is the best case.

Part one

Meet the Men

"You must become an old man in good time if you wish to be an old man long."

Marcus Aurelius

Roman emperor, soldier, philosopher

One

Beginnings

Men are born to succeed, not to fail.
Henry David Thoreau

Jared Grantham, physician/scientist

The Great Depression was not kind to Dodge City, Kansas. The old cow town still had some of its roughness down by the Arkansas River but the saloons were gone, for the most part. Dodge City was dry: hard liquor was not sold. The only alcoholic beverage available on the open market was what was called “three-two” beer, a brew whose alcohol content was limited to three-point-two per cent alcohol, about half what a normal beer contains. Still, the good folks of Dodge City were not entirely without their spirits. Other places were not dry and bottles of whiskey regularly made their way into Dodge and willing gullets.

One of these gullets belonged to Jimmy Grantham, a native son with an outgoing personality and a gift for gab. Jimmy worked as a soda jerk and made deliveries to a beauty salon where a young woman named Ista Taylor worked for her brother. The Taylors had fled hard times in Oklahoma. Jimmy wooed Ista and they were married in 1934, the heart of the Dust Bowl years, when unimaginable clouds of dirt from as far away at Nebraska would sweep across the Great Plains, choking people and animals and coating everything in a fine dust.

Jimmy and Ista managed to hang on to their jobs and live a modest life. On May 19, 1936, they were blessed with a boy they named Jared James. He was born on a fine spring day. Within a month Dodge City would be gripped in heat that topped one-hundred degrees and the young couple and their new baby struggled to find comfort in the decades before air conditioning.

Jared James Grantham would one day become one of the world’s leading kidney researchers, feted in great cities of Europe and Asia and honored at the great universities of North America. But in 1936 he was a child of the Dust Bowl.

Tom Glenn, spy, author

Los Angeles in 1936 was a place of dreams for Americans whose lives lacked glamour and money. It drew dreamers and those seeking sunshine and a better life in much the way it draws them today. On November 23rd of that year Thomas Louis Glenn Junior, a native of Montana, and his wife Grace, a child of West Virginia, welcomed into the world a boy they named Thomas Louis Glenn the Third. Tom the Third would later describe his parents this way: "My mother was an alcoholic and my father was a criminal, a complete bum." Tom Junior was also a lawyer. He embezzled forty-thousand dollars from a client when Tom the Third was twelve. He went to prison, was disbarred, and spent the rest of his life in and out of jail. He died in a bar fight at the age of sixty-nine. His mother, a heavy smoker, would die of lung cancer when her son was middle aged.

Shortly after Tom was born, his parents moved to Oakland. His childhood was not the stuff of children's stories. His older sister died at the age of six of polio. Tom was four at the time. He remembers the war years when GIs and sailors were common in the Bay Area, where military bases had sprung up for the war in the Pacific.

His father was too old for the draft and spent the war working as a private attorney. Not long after the war ended, he went to prison, leaving Tom and his mother to fend for themselves. His mother worked menial jobs and Tom took whatever work a boy could find to help out. He did not do well in school and was told he was slow and not bright. He believed what he was told.

This boy who was written off as having below average intelligence began teaching himself foreign languages at the age of eight, an interest developed through his love of opera. Later in his life he would speak seven languages, earn a PhD, spend thirteen years in and out of Vietnam as a high level intelligence operative, and lecture on opera. And he would publish books.

Grady Smith, career Army officer/ teacher/author

St Louis in the thirties saw itself as a city as important as Chicago. It was "The Gateway to the West" and was still in the afterglow of the 1904 World's Fair formally known as the Louisiana Purchase Exposition. The city had hosted the high and low from all over the world and more than two-hundred-thousand people had been there for the opening of the fair. Time and fortune had slipped away and the Great Depression had sapped vitality out of the middle of the country, but the city still had dreams.

So did O'Neill Grady Smith, a native of North Carolina. His father first took the family to Arizona and what he believed was a healthy climate, but Arizona didn't work out so the family headed east and ran out of money in St. Louis. O'Neill's dad took a job as a streetcar conductor. As a young man O'Neill met and married a local girl named Marie Barron. She was Irish Catholic. He was Baptist, "sort of." They married in the early twenties, had two children, and fifteen years into their marriage, a third child, a boy they named Grady.

Grady's earliest memory is chasing fireflies at the age of three. He was educated in Catholic schools, spent four years in a seminary but gave up his dream of becoming a priest in what he now calls "the death of idealism." He was a theater major in college who spent his career in the military. His time in seminary was followed by a tour in Vietnam as a company commander in an infantry unit in the Mekong Delta. He would retire as a Lieutenant Colonel and return to the arts.

Johnny Holliday, Rock and Roll disc jockey, sportscaster

Miami in 1937 was not the city it is today. It was smaller and in the years before air conditioning it was not attractive as a place to live year-round. But it was home to John and Dorothy Bobbitt. They were both twenty-one and newly married when their first child was born on October 15, 1937. They named him John Holliday Bobbitt, Holliday being Dorothy's maiden name. In some ways Johnny lived an idyllic childhood, playing catch with his dad in the back yard, running shirtless, going to the nearby beaches, and playing sports. But there were dark days that would scar the boy.

His earliest memory is watching a military plane fly low over his house during World War Two and hearing on the radio that the aircraft had crashed into Biscayne Bay. He was six or seven at the time. His father worked for Phillip Morris and travelled throughout Florida, sometimes taking Johnny along. His dad was a champion bowler and boxer.

Johnny played sports in high school; baseball, basketball and football. He was smaller than the other boys but he worked hard at it. His love of sports would carry him through life. He would become one of the most beloved sports broadcasters in the country, enter the Broadcasting Hall of Fame, and garner boxloads of awards. But in his early years he had no idea that a career in broadcasting was even possible.

James King, detective, author

In 1943 Washington, D.C., was a war town. The Second World War needed bureaucrats, planners, secretaries, new government buildings, and anyone who could contribute to the war effort in any way. And, of course, soldiers, sailors and Marines who were working at the War Department or training for combat overseas. One of those soldiers was Quessell King, a native son of Virginia named after a famous French surgeon. Quessell and a local beauty named Marguerite Phelps were married and nine months later they were the proud parents of a boy they named James. He would be their only child. Not long after the boy's arrival, Quessell shipped out to England to train as an anti-aircraft gunner for the invasion of France. As luck would have it, the gun was late in arriving and Quessell missed the initial invasion at Normandy and landed at Omaha Beach thirty days later. He fought across France and into Belgium, taking part in the Battle of the Bulge, and eventually crossing the Rhine River into Germany.

While the war raged in Europe and the Pacific, James "Jim" King and his mother lived with her parents in Southeast Washington. His mother had six brothers; "rowdy" is how Jim describes them. His earliest memory is of his uncles holding him upside down with his feet pressed to the ceiling of his grandmother's house. "Look, the kid walked on the ceiling," they told her. She was, says Jim, "pissed."

His father survived the war and came home to a son he barely knew. He thought the toddler was one of the neighbor's kids. Jim would grow up to become a detective in the Montgomery County, Maryland, police department and investigate and solve one of the county's most notorious crime sprees.

Jim Bohannon, broadcaster

The war touched nearly every family in America in some way. The men who were called to fight were shuffled off to places they would never have visited had they been following the normal course of their lives. Such was the case with Everett and Dorothy Bohannon of Lebanon, Missouri. Everett was sent to Corvalis, Oregon, to train and prepare for combat in the Pacific. Dorothy was pregnant with her second child. Her first child, a boy, had died two years earlier shortly after his birth. In early January of 1944 Dorothy gave birth to a boy the couple named James. Six months later Dorothy and James returned to Lebanon. Everett had health problems that prevented him from shipping out to face the Japanese.

Lebanon was a small town of a few thousand in the northern Ozarks. In the forties it was supported by agriculture. Dorothy's father was a prominent judge in the community. Everett described himself as a "hillbilly" and would spend the post-war years as a travelling salesman.

For James it was a Donna Reed Show kind of place, very pleasant and wholesome. Crime consisted of a few stolen hubcaps or some country boys turning over outhouses on Halloween. Tree-lined streets, lazy summers, small town America as seen in movies. At least that's how James saw it. Jim Bohannon would grow up, develop a big voice, and host a radio program heard by millions of Americans every weeknight.

Lamont Gibson, Federal EEO Director, Air Force Officer

Not every American grew up in ideal small town USA. Children whose skin was black lived in a very different America in those years. In 1944 a nineteen-year old student at Alabama State University discovered that she was pregnant. As was a custom in those years for young girls of any race, her family in Montgomery made her leave town and she was sent to live with relatives in Chicago. In late winter of 1945 she gave birth to a boy she named Lamont. Then she met a man who moved them to Cleveland, where Lamont would grow up. It was a tough city. Gangs, violence, poverty and the menu of deprivation would turn the boy into a hard young man. Before his maturity he saw death, fear, crime and despair close up.

He had one quality that would lift him out of it. He was smart. He enlisted in the Air Force, served in Vietnam, spent a brief time as a police officer in Washington, D.C., and continued his education, obtaining a Master's Degree.

This boy who grew up hard would one day present a resume that includes Federal Agency Director of Equal Employment Programs, Director of Defense Intelligence Agency Attaché Hall of Fame and President and CEO of a real estate investment firm. But on that March morning in 1945 in chilly Chicago, his future was very much in doubt.

Two

"Life is not a problem to be solved, but a reality to be experienced."
Soren Kierkegaard

"In my day" is a phrase that old men typically throw out as they launch into a story about how they had to walk five miles through waist-deep snow to get to school after they had done back-breaking chores. At least that's the stereotype. Some guys probably had to do that. None of the men in this book fit that mold. Their childhood days were in the thirties, forties and fifties. So when they tell stories about their years as kids they are talking about an America without television, air conditioning, or constant fear that somehow children would be harmed if they stepped out into the world to, say, play on their own.

"Go out and don't come back until dinner," was a common order from mothers to sons. Neighborhoods rang with bells, whistles or shouts as parents called their kids home from wherever they had been. And make no mistake, a friend's mom would rat you out in a minute if you broke a window or did something stupid.

The country was on a high in those years. Fathers had won World War Two or fought in Korea and the United States was the most powerful nation the world had ever seen. Millions of men had come home to the GI Bill, gone to college and melded into the middle class. Men who passed on college got good blue collar jobs that paid a living wage and they bought homes in the brand new suburbs.

As our hormones kicked in there was Elvis and Buddy Holly and Little Richard to welcome us to the world of Rock and Roll. We giggled as we squatted under our desks during drills to teach us how to survive a nuclear attack by the dreaded Russians, our lone enemies in the world. We talked endlessly about girls and what mysteries were waiting under those poodle skirts.

By the late fifties Dick Clark was hosting American Bandstand and we came home from school to watch the likes of Frankie Lymon and the Teenagers lip-sync their Top 40 hits. We learned to smoke. We put metal taps on the heels of our shoes to announce to the world that we were cool. We greased our hair with Wild Root and combed it back into ducktail hair styles. We got pimples. We felt breasts. We had part time jobs and bought junker cars that we fixed up in hopes of getting lucky. Some did. Most did not.

Jared Grantham grew up in western Kansas in a part of the country depicted in movies with cowboys and Indians and cattle drives. His first decade or so was spent in Pratt, Kansas, a town spurred by the railroad building in the late nineteenth century. Pratt is two hundred miles, give or take, from the Colorado border and is in the so-called "green" part of the state, where moisture is plentiful. There were about seven thousand people in Pratt at the time. Jared was an active boy, athletic, smart, inquisitive.

His father, Jimmy, worked for a propane company and drove bottles of the gas to the towns in the "brown" part of Kansas, where moisture was scarce. Towns like Liberal, Ulysses, Syracuse and Johnson. Towns that were the dead center of the dust bowl days of the Dirty Thirties. These towns had no sources of energy. Electricity was still on the horizon for places far away from big cities. Propane was the fuel for heat and cooking and the company that employed Jimmy Grantham did very well.

Jimmy was an amiable man who made friends easily. One of his customers owned a furniture store in Syracuse and thought it would be a fine idea to open a satellite store in the town of Johnson, county seat of Stanton County, a seven-hundred square mile section of high plains hard by Colorado. Then, as now, the population of Stanton County was around two-thousand. This store owner thought Jimmy would be the ideal partner to set up shop in Johnson. Jimmy and his wife Ista agreed.

Jared was in the sixth grade when the family moved into an apartment over the store. One of his chores was to empty the chamber pots, given that indoor plumbing was not part of the deal. But there were benefits. The rain had returned to the Dust Bowl and wheat crops were at record levels. The year the Granthams moved to Johnson, the wheat harvest was so large there was no place to store it, so mountains of it were stored by the grain elevators, right on the ground.

As Jared describes it, "It was a high time. People had money. They were in high spirits. They were delighted to have a furniture store come in."

Jimmy Grantham, however charming he was, did not have a natural sense for business. "He couldn't add and subtract very well," says Jared. Jimmy allowed his customers to talk him down in price and so the profits were not what they might have been. Jared's mother, Ista, had no formal business training but she knew how to drive a hard bargain. Within a year the Granthams bought out their partner in Syracuse and moved to a house on the edge of town.

Jared was a strapping boy, tall, strong and handsome. He was a star student. He was also a star athlete. He loved life. He spent nights staring at the star-filled sky over the plains and dreamed. In the summer of 1950 he fell ill. A virus had entered his body. He was diagnosed with polio. It changed everything. He had dreams of playing quarterback for the University of Kansas or playing for the Yankees. As he puts it today, "Polio took all those dreams away."

He lost the use of part of his body and one lung. He became, to use his word, "a cripple." His depression and self-pity gave way to curiosity about music and science and the path to healing others, if not himself. He graduated from high school, went to Baker University and earned an undergraduate degree, and moved on to the University of Kansas medical school.

The mid-twentieth century is not remembered as a golden period for African Americans. Jim Crow laws still ruled life in the Deep South. Northern cities, despite the myth that they were racial Gardens of Eden, were segregated by neighborhood and opportunity. Lamont Gibson, whose mother had been forced to give up her dreams of a college education when she became pregnant with him, spent part of the late forties with his grandfather in Montgomery, Alabama. His grandfather was prominent in the black community and life was good for the boy.

At age five his mother moved to Cleveland with her new husband and Lamont went north. Cleveland in the fifties, says Lamont, was "extremely violent, extremely racist." Socially, he says, it was a struggle to survive. "Kids roamed in gangs. If you wanted to survive, you had to be part of a gang. Neighborhoods were segregated. Doctors, lawyers and Indian chiefs lived in the same approximate area, Shaker Heights. We're up from Shaker Heights. I lived in a more integrated zone. Some gangs were big and they went across the city. Unfortunately, I got involved in that type of gang so I was exposed to a lot of very serious violence. I believe it shaped my life in dealing with people because I was more prone to be extreme than moderate."

But Lamont had something going for him. He was smart and his mother sent him to Catholic schools where the level of education was higher than in the public schools. In fairness it could also be said that he had an element of luck on his side. Despite the social problems that defined his world, he was never arrested by the police. His record was clean. His ticket out of Cleveland was the United States Air Force.

The forties were cruel to Tom Glenn. His father, a lawyer, went to prison when Tom was twelve. Tom and his mother were left poor and alone in Oakland, California. His mother turned to alcohol to deal with her misery. She had been trained as a teacher but chose not to work in that field out of what Tom calls "a shame trip." She worked at a jewelry store taking telephone orders.

Tom was forced to find part-time jobs to make money to help pay the bills. He worked his way through high school and college at Berkeley. He spent a good part of his childhood listening to adults to who told him he was "very dumb" and would probably not amount to much. He believed them and performed poorly in school. He was advised to forget about college because he wasn't bright enough but he managed to get into Berkeley. He did poorly in college, still thinking he was "very dumb" but he graduated with a degree in music. He was not lucky with the girls because he had little self-confidence.

Let's backtrack a bit. This "dumb" kid who everyone agreed would never amount to much spent a good deal of his free time teaching himself foreign languages. When Tom was six years old his parents took him to see the movie *Going My Way*, starring Bing Crosby. There is a scene that features a segment from the opera *Carmen*. This six-year-old was so entranced by the beautiful music he begged his father to buy him the recording. His dad purchased a six-record set of the opera and Tom listened over and over. Carmen is in French. Other operas are in Italian. Tom loved them all and at the age of eight discovered books that helped him learn both languages. He was fascinated by language differences. In high school he learned Latin. In college he learned German. He tried teaching himself Chinese but it was too difficult so he enlisted in the U.S. Army to attend the language school at Monterey, the best in the world. Instead, the army taught him Vietnamese. He had to go to graduate school to learn Chinese.

The National Security Agency took note of his ability to speak French, Vietnamese and Chinese, the primary languages of Vietnam. He would spend the better part of thirteen years as a high level intelligence operative for the NSA. This "very dumb" kid turned out to be very bright.

Part Two

Moving Out of the House

Life can only be understood backwards;
but it must be lived forwards.
Soren Kierkegaard

Three

Launching

"You don't have a home until you leave it and then, when you have left it, you never can go back."

James Baldwin

It is an assumption today that young people won't leave home. Twenty-somethings, the so-called *Millennials*, just don't move out of their parents' basements. Childhood has been extended into the thirties, we're told. Yet even a casual stroll through one of America's thriving downtowns will dispel that idea, given the number of young people who are living on their own. The dividing line would appear to be young people who have the choice of staying at home or moving out – and the financial resources to do so. Meaning, of course, a job.

Fifty years ago the choice was not there. As James King's father put it, "You'll be eighteen. Where you gonna live?"

In the 1960s, many young men did not have college as an option and neither did they have the option of living in Mom and Dad's basement. Get a job and begin life as a grownup, that was the message. The military was often option number one. It was the era of the draft so we all had to go sooner or later.

For Lamont Gibson, it was the Air Force.

For James King, the Navy called. Or rather, waited by the door. James made a half-hearted attempt to attend the University of Maryland. He had to attend an eight-week summer school and do well enough to gain admission. “I was playing in rock and roll bands every Friday and Saturday night, and I worked a part-time job at Sears selling tires and I had a girlfriend. There was a back door of my dormitory that I was in and there was a path through the woods right to the back door of the local bar on Route One. So, needless to say, I slept through a lot of classes. They said, ‘You know, if you don’t drop out now, we’ll flunk you and you will never be able to come to Maryland U. for the rest of your life.’ I said, ‘Oh, well, I’m out of here’.”

Jim King in the Navy

James spent his Navy time on an aircraft carrier in the Mediterranean and the Caribbean. "I loved that stuff," he says. He loved it so much he wanted to extend his enlistment so he could be assigned to an aircraft carrier in the Pacific and visit Japan, the Philippines and Hawaii. But the Vietnam War was heating up. "I was smart enough to know that this didn't bode well for anybody on the West Coast in the Navy."

He got out, hitchhiked home and talked his way back into college. On his first day there he met a "beautiful, tall, thin, pale-skin Irish girl with black hair" named Joanna Pitcher. Three years later they were married.

For Tom Glenn, the kid who was considered slow, or "learning disabled" as we would put it today - the kid who taught himself several languages to better understand the opera he loved - it was off to Berkeley after a childhood of poverty and misery.

"I wanted to be an actor. I found out I wasn't good enough and switched over to music. By the time I graduated I knew I wasn't good enough to be a first-class musician. And I had always been writing, so I went back to writing," Glenn says. Writing, even then, was not a steady paycheck that could pay the rent. The Army beckoned.

"I enlisted so I could go to the language school." He already spoke French, Italian, Latin and German. "I wanted to study Chinese," he says. He enlisted and was sent to the Army Language School at Monterey, California – the best language school in the world - but times were changing. A new cloud was on the horizon. "but they didn't teach me Chinese, they taught me Vietnamese, which was a language I had never heard of." He graduated first in his class and was assigned to the National Security Agency at Ft. Meade, Maryland.

Never one to sit idle and bored, he enrolled at Georgetown University to pick up at Master's Degree in Chinese. He was discharged from the Army in 1962, hired by the NSA and was promptly sent to Vietnam.

For Grady Smith, the seminarian who couldn't face a life of celibacy, the path was similar to Glenn's. College and the Army. The theater major and religious scholar signed up for Officers Candidate School. He went all-in. Basic training as an enlisted man, advanced infantry training, six months of OCS, jump school, Ranger school, and the famed 82nd Airborne Division, then doing duty in the Dominican Republic in something called Operation Power Pack. The United States wanted to make sure that a civil war in that country ended in favor of our guy. President Lyndon Johnson was determined to prevent the country from becoming communist. Remember, this was only three years after the Cuban Missile Crisis.

In addition to the 82nd, Army Special Forces, support units, and U.S. Marines were there to ensure U.S. interests were maintained. Twenty-seven Americans died, thirteen of them 82nd Airborne paratroopers, in an action no one remembers. For Smith, it was just an overture to the biggest Cold War conflict, Vietnam.

For Jared Grantham, the military was not an option. Polio had robbed him of a fully functioning body. It had not robbed him of his fine mind. He boarded a train in western Kansas for a trip to Kansas City, where a relative drove him to Baldwin and a small school called Baker University. He was away from home and on his own. It would change his life. And, in years to come, he would save the lives of thousands of men and women who suffered from kidney disease.

John Holliday Bobbit loved North Miami High School. He is a naturally optimistic, sunny fellow. College was not an option. There was no money for that. "I didn't know what the hell I wanted to do when I got out of high school. Some of my buddies were going to college and I was embarrassed. I couldn't go. What the hell was I gonna do? And you take anything. I worked in the stockroom at a men's store for $45 a week. And then I delivered parts for a Chevrolet company. The biggest thrill was having a white shirt with the word 'Johnny' on the left chest. I thought it was cool."

Four

Luck versus Hard Work

"It's hard to beat a person who never gives up."
Babe Ruth

"So I branched out. I covered a lot of different bases, thinking, well if they hate me doing this, they'll like me doing that. Maybe then I'll win by default"
Johnny Holliday

Success in life is hard to define. It's more than money or prestige and it means different things to people. One man may say he's a success because he has a loving family. Another may think he's a failure because he has only one million dollars and not the ten million he went after. And there's the whole "free lunch" thing in which some individuals believe that the world owes them something and anything less than a free lunch is unfair.

The men in this book are all successful. They have all had disappointments and losses, some of them unbearable. In the end, as they ponder their lives, they each can look in the mirror and see a man who accomplished a great deal.

Johnny Holliday, the Miami kid who didn't have enough money to go to college, is a beloved, even revered, broadcaster. He is also one of the hardest-working men you'll ever meet. Years ago, when he was doing a morning show at WWDC, a radio station in Washington, he would arrive around 5:30 and prepare go to on the air at 6:00. He came ready to entertain, full of energy and comedy bits prepared in advance. He got off the air at 10:00 and spent a couple of hours in the production studio preparing for the next day's show. In the afternoon he was a sought-after commercial announcer. In the evening he starred in local dinner theater productions and got home a little before midnight. Every day. And yet he thinks luck played a role in his success, if only because there was someone around who gave him a chance to show what he could do.

"I think the one thing I never lost sight of is the luck factor has been enormous. Now I know you gotta have a little bit of something going for you, but if you combine that with people giving you a chance, that's all you have to ask for. Then, if you blow it, it's your problem."

Here's an example: Johnny wanted to be a song and dance man, in addition to all of the other things he was doing. So he auditioned for a dinner theater production. He didn't read music.

"So the music director walks to the piano and says, 'Okay, let's run through. What do you want to run through?' I said, 'How about 'The Company Way' from *How to Succeed*?' 'Yeah, sure,' he says, 'What key do you want to do it in?' Well, I don't have an answer because I don't know what key it's in. So I say, 'Key?' 'Yeah, yeah, what key do you want to start off with?' And he knew at that moment that this guy doesn't read music. So he goes ding, ding, ding on the piano. 'Would that be the key?' I say, "Yeah, that's the one right there. Let's do that key.' Then he says, 'How about we take it a notch lower?' Ding, ding. "Yeah, let's do that.' I have no idea." Johnny got the part.

Lamont Gibson will tell you he made his own luck. He not only had to overcome racial discrimination but the low expectations of others. "I think planning is one thing that is very, very important to succeed. But if I was going to tell a young person what to be concerned about, I would tell them to, in order to achieve any goal, you have to do the work. Many people are falsely told you can be anything you want to be. That's not true. If you don't want to do the work, you can't be anything, and you have to have certain skills, and you have to know what they are. If your skill is not reading well, you shouldn't be a lawyer without acquiring the skill to read fast and discuss what you read."

When Gibson was a young man, sadly, his skin color was a door closer. "As a black man I could always be sure that someone is going to jump out of the bushes and stand in the middle of the road and try to prevent me from going forward. I couldn't expect to walk down the road and believe it will be open and clear. Racism in America during my time was so blatant and so conspicuous and obscene, that I knew I couldn't look down the road and say, 'I want to get to a specific point.' I had to set broad goals because I was going to have to change direction." In other words, keep moving but be prepared to change your direction if roadblocks turn up.

And let's not forget Tom Glenn, the kid who was told he was too stupid to do much in life. He began teaching himself languages as a child because he wanted to know what was happening in those operas.

Or Jared Grantham, the athletic kid who contracted polio and could never play sports again. He used his brain and his drive to become a world renowned medical researcher. One could argue that he had the "luck" to be born with unusual intelligence. How then to explain his extraordinary drive and determination to use it?

Anyone over the age of thirty knows someone who had great talent and allowed it to fade into failure. Alcohol, drugs, laziness, selfishness and general lack of ambition can all sap whatever talents a man had the "luck" to be born with.

Chapter five

Success

"Action is the foundation to all success."
Pablo Piccaso

"Don't ever think you can't do something."
Johnny Holliday

Johnny Holliday may be the most relentlessly optimistic person in this book. He is quick to praise others and reluctant to claim credit. "You have to have confidence. You have to have that stuff. I always thought I could do anything." It's worked for him. If anyone asks Johnny if he can do something, anything, the answer is always yes. "If you say no, someone else is gonna get it."

Young Johnny Holliday

He acknowledges that the key is being asked. "I got the first disc jockey job by accident. And when I look back, if that thing doesn't happen, if the guy doesn't give me a shot, then I don't know where I'd be today. And I think that's what is a major contributor for somebody, for an older person to give a younger person just the opportunity and maybe see something in them."

First jobs are often humbling experiences. The new guy gets the job nobody else will take. It's just how it works. Take it or leave it.

A man named Al Evens owned a small radio station in Perry, Georgia. Radio at its most basic. He offered Johnny a job. "Thirty-two bucks a week. Daytime station. You can sign it on. Come back at noon. We do a show called the Stumpus Family. I'm the host, my wife plays the piano, the chief engineer plays this character, you can play little Johnny Stumpus." So Johnny, aka Johnny Stumpus, begins his career in radio. He signs the station on in the morning and plays records until nine o'clock. He comes back at noon to be part of the Stumpus family show, which Johnny describes as "godawful," then he comes back at night to play recordings of the Lawrence Welk Show, and then string music on a show called "Dream Awhile" until he signed off. Thirty-two dollars a week. Not much, even then.

He got an idea that would, in time, send him to the top of play-by-play announcers in America and make him a legend in Washington-area sports. "I convinced them to let me do the high school basketball games." Al Evens agreed but only if Johnny could find a sponsor. He did. "So I take a big tape recorder and sit in the stands and broadcast the game. Since it was a daytime station we would play it back the next day. I got an extra twenty-five dollars for that."

Today Johnny is the longtime play-by-play man for the University of Maryland men's football and basketball teams. He's paid more than twenty-five dollars per game.

Crediting others is important to Lamont Gibson. He struggled with racism as a young man but he acknowledges that white people with good hearts made great contributions and improved racial attitudes and laws to make the country better in the years since his youth. "It is important to remember that it was an all-white House and Senate that passed the 13th and 14th Amendments to our Constitution abolishing slavery and guaranteeing due process and equal rights to all Americans citizens. It was a white House and Senate that passed the 1964 Civil Rights Act that prohibited discrimination in employment, voting, public accommodations, public facilities and public education."

White, high-ranking officers helped him become an officer in the Air Force Reserve and helped move him up in the ranks. This kind of assistance was only an opportunity. He had to deliver. Just like Johnny Holliday and everyone else, opportunity is not the same as success. That comes with hard work.

"Surround yourself with successful people. Avoid the voice of people who are not successful because they will bring you down. If you have people around you who are constantly failing, they will cause you to fail," Lamont says.

Lamont got to know the legendary Marine General Paul Xavier Kelly, known in the Corp as P.X. Kelly. Lamont was working as a civilian at the Quantico Marine Corps Development and Education Commanding General's staff at the time. General Kelly rose through the ranks at lightning speed and got his first star at the age of forty-six. Nine years later he was Commandant of the Marines.

After Kelly's promotion to Brigadier General, Lamont had the guts to pull him aside and ask him about his success. "What was it that got you here?" he asked. "Well, I put my troops first. I work all day taking care of my troops, all night doing paperwork, all that has to be done to get the job done," Kelly replied. That, Lamont says, and "not being afraid to work fourteen, sixteen, eighteen hours a day." That's the key to success. He got around obstacles, seized his opportunities, and made the most of them.

Jared Grantham had his obstacles but he, too, found a way around them. Despite having been, to use his word, "crippled" from polio, he went to medical school and did well. He took a fellowship at the National Institutes of Health. Then he took a fellowship in England. As a fledgling researcher he made very little money. He was given opportunities to work with the best minds and he made the most of it.

Tom Glenn also climbed an arduous road. A difficult childhood could have left him by the side of the road like so many other young men and women who decide that the ditch life hands them is too steep to climb out of. He put himself through college, found a way to learn languages, performed at the top of the heap wherever he was. He spent thirty-five years working for the National Security Agency and even today the details of his service are not revealed. At each step of his journey he seized the chance to move up. Granted, he was blessed with rare intelligence, but many very smart people squander their gifts and never make it out of where they began.

These days Tom is a writer, choosing to spend most of his time alone. His book, *The Last of the Annamese*, is a great work of art. The book is about the last days of Saigon as the North Vietnamese were ending the war by smashing what we left behind, including the South Vietnamese army. It contains previously classified details that offer new light into the days leading up to the moment when the North Vietnamese tanks crashed through the gates of the Presidential Palace.

This is only one of his books. Tom is driven to write, to express himself on paper. "All I can tell you is that there's a subliminal urge in me that I can't control, even if I try to control it, that pushes me into writing. I just can't help it. It's not about getting published, not about readers, it's the writing itself. And it's just irresistible. I can't stop doing it."

All of the men whose stories you are reading have been successful. All of them began their adult years facing challenges. All of them were helped in some way and they all took advantage of the opportunities they were given. They all worked their asses off.

Part Three

War and Race

"Only the dead have seen the end of war."
Plato

The American Negro never can be blamed for his racial animosities - he is only reacting to 400 years of the conscious racism of the American whites.
Malcolm X

Six

Vietnam

"I am afeard there are few die well that die in battle, for how can they charitably dispose of anything when blood is their argument?"
William Shakespeare, Henry V

"I had Delta Company"
Grady Smith

Men in their seventies today are living in the backdraft of two events that shaped the generation. One is the civil rights movement. The other is Vietnam. For many African Americans Vietnam is an extension of the civil rights movement. Racial tensions at home were mirrored in the military units fighting the war. Some black soldiers refused to fight, saying they had no quarrel with Asians.

For white men, the war was the defining element of their young lives. Four of the seven men whose stories are being told in this book went to Vietnam. Three are white. For the fourth, Lamont Gibson, the civil rights struggle straddled his time "in-country."

The Vietnam War was a decade-and-a-half mistake that cost nearly sixty-thousand American lives and Vietnamese casualties numbering a million or more. No one knows exactly how many men, women and children perished. The United States supported South Vietnam. The Soviet Union and its allies provided aid to North Vietnam. After all of the fighting and domestic turmoil in the U.S., we lost. I won't get into all of the arguments why one should or should not have supported the war. That ground has been raked many times. In the end, most Americans came to oppose the war and feelings of bitterness still linger.

Those who fought were sometimes subjected to harassment, humiliation, and even spit when they returned. They not only had to deal with the horrors and fear they had endured, they had to process the hatred of some of their countrymen.

Tom Glenn, NSA undercover, Vietnam

Let's begin with Tom Glenn, whose time in Vietnam was greatest. I will note here that today Tom suffers from what he calls "post-traumatic stress injury." He believes that "injury" is more accurate than "disorder" to describe the condition in which past traumatic events interrupt later life.

As noted, Tom speaks the three primary languages in Vietnam. He loves the culture of the country and has written it into some of his books. He worked in signals intelligence, grabbing enemy information by intercepting communications. It provided valuable information for American and South Vietnamese forces. It was intense, dangerous work. It required him to spend extended periods of time with Vietnamese.

"I lived in it," he said. "I was right smack in the midst of it. The only way to survive was to do what they did. Eat the way they did. Sleep the way they did. Shit the way they did, quite frankly." Vietnamese is a very difficult language for Americans to learn because it is structured differently. The structure of the language is infused into the culture. Tom found it all very attractive.

Did he like the Vietnamese? "I loved them and still do," he said. Most of the people he dealt with were soldiers, "down to earth people."

The war ended badly for the U.S. and the South Vietnamese. In 1975 the North Vietnamese stormed across the Demilitarized Zone, overwhelmed the South Vietnamese Army, and took over the south, crashing into Saigon, the capital, and renaming it Ho Chi Minh City after the man who had led the move to unify Vietnam. Many American allies were abandoned. One of Tom's South Vietnamese friends, an army major, refused to evacuate and chose to shoot his wife and children, then himself. "He was a fine man," says Tom. "There were many like that."

Tom had great respect for the South Vietnamese as soldiers and, at the time, he believed in the war against the communists. He admits, however, that we should never have gone to war there. Ho Chi Minh, he points out, came to the United States and asked for help to drive the French out after World War Two. We sided with the French, who were then driven out by Ho and his fighters. We stepped in and suffered the same fate.

Tom is left with his memories of friends and the horrors of war.

Grady Smith, infantry company commander, Vietnam

Grady Smith was a young army officer at Ft. Bragg in North Carolina when his first child, a daughter, was born. Six weeks later he, his wife and their new baby drove across country to Fort Lewis, Washington where Grady, a first lieutenant waiting for promotion to captain, would train with his new unit for deployment to Vietnam. Shortly after the Tet Offensive of 1968, Grady's unit was sent to what he calls "the soft underbelly of Saigon" to join the 9th Infantry Division. Army leadership was fearful of another massive communist offensive.

Tet was a watershed for the war. In 1968 the Viet Cong, the guerrilla movement in the south, and the North Vietnamese Army, the NVA, rose up and attacked everywhere across South Vietnam, causing massive casualties and a shock to the confidence of the United States that we were winning the war. The communists suffered catastrophic casualties and the Viet Cong were all but wiped out, but the damage was done. After Tet the American war effort turned to finding a way out.

Grady was a captain and had been assigned as the battalion's intelligence officer, the guy who processed and briefed the commanders about whatever was known about the enemy.

Decisions in wartime conditions are not always smart. Another captain in the battalion, a company commander, made a mistake that got him wounded. As Grady puts it, "He found a cache of homemade grenades that the local VC had put together and he brought them in in an empty sandbag sack and the damn thing exploded. He was coming in for a meeting called by the battalion commander and he almost wiped out the whole command structure. He damn near lost his leg when that thing went off. They stabilized him. They medevaced him to Japan." The captain eventually healed and returned to Vietnam. "But he had a desk after that."

And Grady had a rifle company to command. It was a straight infantry unit. “Either we walked or we got helicopters from Rent-A-Chopper.” The company was seventy-five to eighty per cent authorized strength. “Mostly the NVA were intercepted and challenged en route down. We had a few firefights, enough to bloody the battalion, enough to get people used to being shot at and shooting back. If we had been up in I Corp it would have been a much more busy war for us.” I Corp, pronounced “Eye Core,” was in the northern part of Vietnam was fighting was heaviest.

1968 was a rough year for the country. Tet drove away dreams of victory in Vietnam. Martin Luther King Jr. and Robert Kennedy were murdered. Cities burned in rage and riot. Anti-war protesters took to the streets by the hundreds of thousands to protest the draft and the war. That summer the Democratic National Convention in Chicago turned into what one report called “a police riot” as cops went after protesters.

All of this was not lost on the men who were fighting and dying in the jungles of Southeast Asia. Discipline in the ranks was fraying. Marijuana and other drugs were easily available and some of Grady’s troops were using these substances to ease their war experience. But the race problems back home were like a cancer in the ranks.

“There were some racial issues that came out really, really big,” Grady says. “I had that company when Robert Kennedy was assassinated. I had that company when Martin Luther King was assassinated.” The turmoil in America sobered Grady.

“We were at two-thousand feet in choppers waiting to go into an objective area that was being prepped by the artillery for us. We could see all the puffs of smoke down there laying in. And the word came down the channel that Robert Kennedy had died. And I’m thinking, like, what the hell are we doing here with that going on at home.”

Jim Bohannon, intelligence analyst, Vietnam

For Jim Bohannon, Vietnam was a given, even though the Army played a little game of promising that a good performance in the Army Security Agency School at Fort Devens, Massachusetts, would allow him to choose his assignment. During the draft days many young men chose to enlist under the promise that they would avoid assignment to the infantry in the jungles of Southeast Asia. Such duty would be the lot of draftees, those who had to be forced into the service for two years to fulfill their military obligation.

Jim went to the recruiter in his hometown of Lebanon, Missouri, and did well enough on the required tests that the recruiter told him about the super-secret Army Security Agency, a signals intelligence unit that required high test scores to even apply. So off he went to the ASA school where he did well. "You got three choices to put down. Everybody knew that just about everybody was going to Vietnam. My class had twenty-eight guys in it. Twenty-six of them went to Vietnam." Including Jim. "The guessing game was what assignment do you put down so that you have a shot at not going to Vietnam. Of two who did not go, one went to Panama and the other guy went to Hawaii."

Jim's signal intelligence unit supported an infantry brigade. Photos of him during that period show a skinny young man wearing black framed glasses standing outside a sandbag bunker. He worked as an intelligence analyst and had planned to extend beyond his one-year assignment because the army was offering an extra thirty-days of leave to those who stayed in Vietnam an additional six months. He gave up that idea after Tet and came home.

Lamont Gibson, Air Force enlisted man, Vietnam

For Lamont Gibson the military was a different experience. In 1964 he decided to join the Air Force. He wanted to get into the new field of computers. "The Air Force said, 'We don't need computer operators. We need firemen. We need police officers.'" He went to Basic Training where he was made a squad leader because he had been in the Boy Scouts. That allowed him to march other trainees around the base. The Air Force, he says, was not always fair to African Americans at the time and he had a "four and no more" attitude, meaning he would do his four years and get out. His first assignment was Wurtsmith Air Force Base outside Oscoda, Michigan, as an Air Force Police Officer, or AP.

"It appeared that only blacks were going to jail," he says. Why? "Because they were black. They were going to ruin your record. Many blacks on the base complained of getting an Article 15 or some punishment that would have a negative impact on their records." Article 15 is a written punishment for violation of a military rule or regulation. At that time, it prevented the military person from getting a promotion or an award for one year.

Then came Da Nang Air Force base in Vietnam. "Blacks and whites lived and died together in wooden huts. When the mortars would come in and kill guys, we had to pick up the body parts and put them in body bags. Some of the guys would pick up the body parts and throw in a limb here and a limb there in the body bags without caution or consideration. You'd end up with a white leg or arm with a black body."

He finished his four-year Air Force duty at Andrews AFB near Washington where, he says, a white commander refused to award him a commendation that he earned in Vietnam because he was black. Another white Air Force NCO (Non-Commissioned officer) gave him a copy of the commendation recommendation so he could have proof that it was to be awarded. By that time, Lamont was so disgusted with the Air Force that he got out. He would later join the Air Force Reserve and become an officer.

Black troops in Vietnam were angry and on occasion refused to fight. It happened to Grady Smith while he was commander of an infantry company. "One of my black troops came in and said he's not going out in the field." This was after a racial incident in the United States that had made the news. "He said he's just not going to do it. He's had enough. My First Sergeant was going to chop his head off. I said let's buy time. We don't have to draw a line in the sand now. About a week or so later we got another mission and we had to go out. This guy was adamant that he was not going out. One of the last things I did as commander was have my First Sergeant prepare failure to repair charges on this guy. I gave him as much leeway as I could, you know, but you gotta do the mission." Failure to repair can be a serious charge in wartime. It means a man has refused to fight.

Blacks and whites, many of them anyway, saw the mission differently. For men like Lamont Gibson it meant fighting the Viet Cong and fighting racism. For Grady Smith, it was going into the field to fight a war he had come to believe was not justified. Today both men and others like them live in retirement and when they look into the mirror they see the men they once were and know they did what they believed they had to do. But even now the distant sound of bugles calls them to their memories.

Part Seven

Race

"As a nation, we began by declaring that 'all men are created equal.' We now practically read it 'all men are created equal, except negroes.'"
Abraham Lincoln

"I saw the restrooms and water fountains for whites only. I rode on the Alabama buses with the white line for blacks to sit in the back of the bus."
Lamont Gibson

It is a shameful fact that from the 1880s to the 1960s segregation was legal in America. From the end of Reconstruction after the Civil War until the great Civil Rights Movement of the 50s and 60s, white people, men mostly, could do pretty much anything they wanted to people of color and it was legal in parts of the South. Legal in the sense that a black person could be arrested for sitting in the front of a public bus or using a whites-only bathroom. A black family traveling through the South could not stay in hotels designated as whites-only. Black families could not live in certain neighborhoods, even in the North. Many northern union jobs were whites-only. Blacks were expected to "know their place," meaning they were told to accept second-class status in the country of their birth.

Even veterans were sent to the sidelines of American life. Black units had performed heroically during World War Two but their country offered them only a slap in the face when they came home. In 1946 a black veteran named Isaac Woodard was blinded while he was in uniform. His crime? Being black.

That is the America the men in this book grew up in. In much the way all children accept the world around them, these men accepted segregation as the way things are, and led their own lives.

Young Lamont Gibson

Of all of the men whose stories are being told in this book only Lamont Gibson has lived out the dramatic change of the past fifty years and personally experienced what America has become from what it was when he was a boy. His mother's family lived in Montgomery, Alabama, where blacks and whites were segregated in every sense of the word. His grandfather was a prominent member of the black community and lived in a big house in an all-black area. Race relations reflected the attitudes of the Old South. Blacks could not cross certain lines and, as Lamont tells us, his grandfather would not allow whites in his house. As bad at Alabama was at that time, Lamont's experience in Montgomery was not as hidden as it was in Cleveland, Ohio, where racism was more a part of everyday life.

"I went to segregated schools and so I knew how racist things were, but I guess my first rude awakening was when I was in elementary school. I went to a Catholic elementary school. One of the valedictorians – young, black and female – wanted to go to a Catholic high school with boys and girls, and they wouldn't let her because at that time, back in the early sixties, even Catholic schools were segregated. The all-boys schools had blacks and white, the all-girl schools had blacks and whites, but the high schools that had boys and girls were all white. They didn't allow black girls and black boys to go to the all-white schools. Some of the nuns were racist and the priests had racist attitudes, some of them."

As a young man in Vietnam, he found racism as onerous as it was on the streets of Cleveland or Montgomery. His career would later find him in a high level position in the federal government fighting discrimination in hiring.

For many men of that generation racism was part of life. Most Americans were not overtly racist, at least not in their own minds, but blacks "over there" and whites "over here" was how it was. Grady Smith remembers St. Louis when he was young. "There were very clear areas where they (blacks) lived. I remember going to school in the early sixties at St. Louis U. and riding across Grand Avenue, a section of town called Mill Creek Valley. It was very slummy. My recollection was that it was basically black."

But America changed. The military changed. "When I got to the Pentagon for my tour in 1980, I knew integration had been institutionalized because I was walking down the Pentagon Mall, down where all those shops are, and a black two-star general walked past me and I knew him by name. He was not an oddity. He was part of the scene," Grady says.

Jared Grantham's boyhood in rural Kansas was a world of white people with a few Hispanics on the margins. "I was a touch racist in that I never lived with any black people." Baker University was mostly white. He also admits to being prejudiced against Jews and homosexuals at that time in his life. He, like most older Americans, says he has evolved in a positive way and he says he has worked hard to establishment friendships with people of color and describes the Kidney Institute at the University of Kansas Medical Center as "a temple of diversity."

Jim Bohannon grew up in Lebanon, Missouri, a small farming community in the northern Ozarks. Lebanon was not in the Deep South and did not have laws that segregated blacks from whites, but it was not fully integrated, either. Race relations were, as he puts it, cordial.

"You didn't have things like lynching or anything like that, but they (blacks) definitely 'knew their place,' which was the north side of town, old town. There was no integration in housing. Of course there was integration in the schools."

"Honestly, I found out what race relations were like when I was back from college one time. Some of my classmates, also back from college, went to the Methodist church, which was a wonderful, very liberated church. My old scoutmaster had gone to that church and had gotten into a Sunday school discussion with the men of the church. My friends, who were like nineteen, I guess, had the temerity to suggest that blacks were equal and were not inferior to whites. Not exactly what you would call cutting edge racial statements, and they were being hooted out of class. They set up a debate for the following week. Since I was a debater, I was invited to be there as an honorary Methodist for a Sunday. Of course, we cleaned their clocks and didn't convince one of them. And that was revealing in that I realized that being a white person, I hadn't thought much about it, but there was a strong current of racism underneath."

All was not hopeless in Lebanon, as it turned out. A very popular athlete who happened to be black was elected student body president.

Indifferent probably best describes the attitude of most white people during the middle of the twentieth century. They were not actively racist nor did they take to the streets to protest the conditions under which their black fellow citizens were living. In a very real sense, the race agenda was set by white people who benefited from the status quo or, in the case of hard core racists, from the fires of their own hatred toward anyone who didn't look like them. America today is much more open to diversity than it was in the 1950s and 60s. Racial discrimination is still a cancer but there is no doubt that minorities have more rights today than they did fifty years ago.

Part Four

Loss and Grief

"Everyone can master a grief but he that has it."
William Shakespeare

Seven

Grief

"If I should meet thee
After long years,
How should I greet thee?
With silence and tears."
Lord Byron

"She was six when she got it. She was nine when she passed away, which was a horrible, miserable time for us."
James King

Three of the seven men in this book have lost children. One also lost his wife. Others lost marriages, idealism, innocence, a sense of safety. Loss is part of life, we're told, and it's true. Does loss hold lessons for us or just leave us devastated? Some losses never go far from our thoughts. Others slip away in time. "Healing" is an overused word that can seem empty to someone just looking for a way to grieve. Sadness can become a companion that never leaves.

Let's begin with James King. His beautiful daughter, Deanna, his first born, contracted brain cancer when she was six years old. Take time to think about the moment when James and his wife were introduced to every parent's nightmare. If you are a parent, try to imagine that moment without choking. No matter how horrible you think it would be, it's worse.

"Losing a child is . . . is . . . was the most difficult time of my life. The hardest thing that ever happened to me was losing my daughter, the first born, the apple of my eye, as they say, a beautiful, smart child. To, you know, be with her, holding her head when she's throwing up from chemotherapy every just, just, I mean, it just . . . it just tore us apart. My wife, Joanna, was just as involved as I was, and maybe more so, because, well, she's the mother and I could go to work, but she didn't. She stayed home all the time with our daughter, so it was probably more difficult for her than it was for me."

These tragedies often cause marriages to end because couples cannot bear to be around each other after the loss of a child. For James King and his wife, it was a bonding.

"It didn't pull us apart, it probably pulled us together. But I did see, while we were at Children's Hospital, fathers that walked away from their sick children and families, couldn't take it, or it was just too much trouble. And I could never understand how a father could walk away from a child. It was always the mother who stayed, although sometimes it was both the mother and father who would walk away and leave the child alone."

Think about that for a moment. Think about a sick child, a dying child, whose parents walk away. There is no greater betrayal. No greater loss. This man, this good man, whose precious daughter was throwing up from chemotherapy, a child whose left side was paralyzed from brain surgeries, who would have given anything for his daughter's health, watched as others walked away from their own precious children.

"It was horrifying. I mean, the child ultimately was the one betrayed. I just . . . it was . . . I don't know. I can't explain it."

James had two other children who brought him great joy and happiness, a son and daughter. He loved his wife and family. But loss was not finished with him. It took the love of his life.

"She had been having some stomach problems, we had gone to the doctor. Tests were done. I was there when he told her. He said, 'It looks like you have cancer.'" Once again he watched a cherished family member undergo chemotherapy and surgery. Two rounds. The first seemed to work for a year or so. But the cancer returned. "She got a staph infection and I took her down to the Washington Hospital Center. She got admitted through the ER. The staph infection could not be controlled." He and their two children stayed at her bedside for two weeks. They didn't want her to die alone.

Me: "What were the conversations the two of you had when she was sick?"

James: "Well, we were very hopeful. I realized the only thing she had, and I think she realized this, was her what would you say? her hope. The hope that everything would be all right. My wife was a religious person and prayed."

Me: "Was she Catholic?"

James: "Yes."

Me: "What about you, your own beliefs? Are you a believer?"

James: "No. Never have been."

Me: "So you didn't rail against God because…"

James: "Because that wasn't an option."

Near the end, as he sat by her bedside, he watched as the ICU's brainwave monitor levelled and went flat. There was no brain activity for two days. This woman who had been his life partner for forty-one years, his best friend, the mother of his children, who had been through the loss of their daughter, was no longer there. His anguish was indescribable, unbearable. He knew he had to let her go. "Truly the hardest decision of my life," he says. "I did not ask my children for their opinion. I did not want them to feel any responsibility for their mother's death. When the ventilator was turned off, she continued to breath on her own for another day." It was good, he says, that he had a few more hours with her. "I was holding her hand when she died. It was tough. Tough."

Grief consumed him. "It was hard. It's like, the only way I've been able to describe it . . . if you're right handed and suddenly you lose it, somehow, in an accident, you have to learn to do everything with your left hand. And you're rather clumsy at first, but as time goes on, you become more adept, but it takes a while to get good with your left hand. It took a year or two. Actually I'm still learning."

Looking back at his decision to have the ventilator turned off, he says, "I would hope if I was in the same situation someone would do it for me."

~~~~

Jared Grantham knew about loss from an early age. Polio had robbed him of a fully functioning body. His inner strength, his drive, helped him find the love of his life, get through medical school, and father four children, the youngest of whom was named Joel. Joel had an engineer's mind and was studying at the University of Kansas when he and three companions were killed when their car was hit by a train in March of 1987. Joel was twenty years old. His loss is still too painful for Jared's wife, Carol, to discuss.
~~~~

Jared's eyes tear up even today when Joel's passing is mentioned.

In March of 1987 Jared's father was dying of cancer in a small hospital in Johnson, Kansas, a farming community in the far western part of the start, not far from the Colorado line. Jared and Carol were living in Bethesda, Maryland, outside Washington, while he was on a research sabbatical at the National Institutes of Health.

"The phone rang at two o'clock in the morning and we thought, he's gone. We got on the phone and it was Aaron (a son) and he was sobbing. He said, 'Dad, Joel's dead.' I said, 'What? Are you sure?' He said, 'Yes, he was killed in a train wreck earlier this evening.' He was beside himself. He was having trouble expressing himself. He gave me the number of a police officer that I could contact for details. Carol was awake and beside herself. I called the policeman. I asked him, do you have absolute proof that it was him? Do you have his billfold? Yes, we have it, he said."

Jared and Carol booked an early flight out of Washington and were back in Kansas City by eight that morning. He and his two surviving sons drove to the crash site. There were newspaper and television reporters on the scene, making notes and taking pictures.

"The TV people took a picture of us where Joel's body had been found. We huddled around that place thinking about him. We finally got our wits about us and went back to campus to pick up his clothes and other effects and brought them home."

This was Jared's dark night of the soul. It collapsed his remaining faith in God. The loss grabbed his mind and sent him into a spiral of grief that could only be relieved if he threw himself into his work, his research. "It was at night that things were difficult, trying to keep my mind from this horrible tragedy. This young man in the prime of his youth, probably our best kid, he did everything by the book. He had a math brain. He was in engineering. I wondered, why did this have to happen to him. Two seconds and he would have been free. Think about it. Two extra seconds and they would have been through that crossing. Why, why, why? I was struggling with my own sense of religion at that moment. I'm a scientist and I was kind of going off on spirituality without being religious. This was a seminal moment in my life. I figured that there's no way in anybody's thinking that a quote God could let something like that happen; an interventional God that people pray to, to save them from floods and wars and pestilence. There's no way a well-meaning God could let something like this happen. Any chance for me to be a religious believer ended at that point, was dashed forever."

Joel died on March 27th. Jared's father died three days later. Losing a parent is a natural part of the order of life. Losing a child is not. "Periodically, like on his birthday, I do grieve. I just sit down and have a good cry, let it hang out. That's healthy, I think."

One beautiful spring morning not long after Joel died Jared and Carol went to the verdant campus of NIH to listen to the cicadas sing, to sit on the grass, and read. Words came to him in that moment. The words became a poem called "Spirit of Mt. Oread." Mt. Oread is a hill upon which the University of Kansas is located. Jared dedicated the poem to all of the precious young people at the university who left this life while they were students. Part of it reads:

If life should end,
Before they've trod,
On down the hill,
Received the nod,
Will they belong
Among the best?
Will memories fade,

As their souls rest?

"Do not despair,
Your child is here.
We are at peace,
We know no fear.
We will enjoy
Eternal youth
Upon this hill,
That is the truth."

There are losses in life that are too painful to recall, too painful to see, like looking directly at the sun. Lamont Gibson lost a son when the young man was in his twenties. It is something he will not discuss.

Part Five

The Work They Did

"All happiness depends on courage and work."
Honoré de Balzac

Nine

Speaking to America

"I'm not qualified to do a heck of a lot.
It's either this or welfare."
Jim Bohannon

There's probably no question a young person hates more than, "What do you plan to do with your life?" Most twenty-year-olds have no clue. It brings to mind the famous scene from *The Graduate* when the young college graduate was being advised to go into plastics by an inebriated older family friend. Instead, the young man, played by Dustin Hoffman, put on some scuba gear and sank to the bottom of the family pool to get away.

None of the men in this book went into plastics. Some had a vague notion of what they wanted to do when the adult world came calling, some made it up as they went along. All of them had ambition. Over these next few chapters you will learn how these men made a living and what it was like for them.

Jim Bohannon as a young broadcaster

Jim Bohannon, the kid from Lebanon, Missouri, was drawn to radio. He worked at local stations when he was in high school and in college. After a stint in Vietnam he worked in local radio while he was finishing his Army hitch. One opportunity led to another and today he speaks to millions of people very night. His work load is a bit easier these days because he lives on a lake in South Carolina and broadcasts his three-hour show from his home. But for years his work day ran to ten hours or more.

"I'd get up around eight in the evening and be out the door before nine. I'd get into work around nine-thirty and be on the air from ten pm until one am. I had done most of my work preparing for the show the previous day. From one in the morning to five I would write a daily feature, record commercials and promotional announcements and then anchor a show called "America in the Morning" from five to six and, depending on events in the news, would we update the show at six and eight in two refeeds and my day would be done. I would go home and be up awhile and I would be in bed around eleven."

So much for the glamour of radio. To succeed, it's hard work and preparation. "You're never unaware of the fact that you're talking to a whole lot of people," he says. Audience surveys over a number of years show that his listeners are "better than average income, better than average education."

Are they driving or at home? "By virtue of my hours they are stationary and probably at home or at work. We do have people who call in who are on the road. Truckers call in."

Until he moved to South Carolina, Jim worked out of studios at the CBS bureau in Washington, where famous and powerful people are often eager to be on the air talking to large audiences about whatever truth they're selling. Actors and singers come through town and they, too, are available for interviews. This kid from a small Midwestern town is not only talking to millions of Americans, he's also talking to names in lights. What's that like?

"Getting hugged by Loretta Lynn was nice. So was getting hugged by Carol Channing. I enjoyed talking to George Foreman." Notice not one Washington A-lister was mentioned at the top of his list.

And not all of his interviews have gone well. The Tass news agency was the mouthpiece for the Soviet Union when it was a Cold War rival to the United States. Jim invited the Tass White House correspondent on the show. "He tried to take over the show and bully me. That turned into a shouting match."

He interviewed Hector "Macho" Commacho, the boxer, who turned out to be a terrible guest. "He wasn't much of a talker. I could not get a response out of him on anything. Finally I got to other boxers in his weight class, Aaron "The Hawk" Pryor and Ray "Boom Boom" Mancini. I asked him, 'What would you say to those who feel that Pryor or Mancini would beat you?' He uttered a few sentences. He said, 'I can beat Pryor. I can beat Mancini. I can beat you.' I said, 'I will give you one out of three. You can beat me.'"

There is nothing worse for a talk show host than a guest who will not provide answers that are longer than yes and no. If the guest is booked for an hour, the endless yes and no answers can seem like a lifetime and the host can almost hear the listeners changing stations. Such was the case with Dr. Edward Teller, known throughout the world as the father of the H-bomb.

"I was told he was a prickly interview. Perhaps that was one syllable too many." Jim knew he had work to do to get through the hour. "We're lay people," he told Heller. "Tell us, how do you make an H-bomb. We don't want details but how do you make one?" Heller wouldn't respond. "It was like trying to pull a tusk out of a hippopotamus."

Jim had been told that Heller hated to be called The Father of the H-bomb. Jim set off a bomb of his own. "I said, Dr. Teller, is it true that every June the H-bomb sends you a Father's Day card? Well, he sputtered a little bit and before you knew it I couldn't shut him up. I asked him, how come we always hated taking physics? 'Because they teach it all wrong. They should call it life,' he said."

When Jim was growing up in Lebanon there were maybe five-thousand people in the town. It was several hours by car from St. Louis and Kansas City. It was not the center of the known world. Now, here he was, in the Nation's Capital, chatting it up with the high and mighty.

"It was heady, to say the least. There were some people for whom I felt like being in hero worship mode. William F. Buckley, for example. I had read him for years. A phenomenal intellect. I interviewed him four or five times." Off the air, the relationship became Jim and Bill.

"It doesn't ever get blasé he says," of being around the rich, powerful and famous. But "they put their pants on one leg at a time. I didn't come away from talking to any of them and saying, wow, I've been in the presence of a god-like being. They are not perfect by any stretch of the imagination."

Ten

Life as a Spy

"Study after study has shown that human behavior changes when we know we're being watched."
Edward Snowden, NSA contractor and international fugitive

"People at NSA are not the least interested in anybody's private life."
Tom Glenn

There may be no more misunderstood line of work than intelligence. The most obvious reason is that the work is classified. The people who actually do the work can't talk about it. The public impression is shaped by leaks, which may not be accurate, and by speculation, often in the movies or books. To be sure, field agents sometimes find themselves in tight spots and on occasion they are killed, wounded or captured. But the day-in-day-out work of spies can be tedious and is, most assuredly, time consuming.

Young Tom Glenn

Tom Glenn spent his working life at the National Security Agency, a government operation that for decades was so secret the federal government wouldn't even admit that it existed. In recent years the NSA has come to symbolize government intrusion in our private lives. After all, its job is to gather intelligence using electronic means. Tom discounts that our private lives are under surveillance because, as his experience has shown, there's too much work to be done gathering information on bad guys to worry about the daily lives of ordinary citizens.

His intelligence career began in the late fifties when he enlisted in the Army on the promise that he could learn Chinese at the Army Language School at Monterey, California, then and now known as the finest language school in the world. He signed up to learn Chinese. He was instead assigned to learn Vietnamese, a language he had never heard of.

For one year he was in class six hours a day, followed by two hours of study. Each day he had to memorize two or three pages of Vietnamese dialogue. He learned to speak it, write it and read it. He graduated at the top of his class and assumed he was to be sent to Vietnam. Instead, he was assigned to the NSA at Ft. Meade, Maryland, where his work was classified. He had evenings off so he enrolled at Georgetown University where he learned Chinese. He already spoke French. He was now fluent in the three principle languages of Southeast Asia.

His enlistment over, he was offered a job at NSA at a GS11 rank, an unusual starting position. In his new job with his new pay grade he was promptly sent to Vietnam where he would be in and out of the country for the next thirteen years. He was one of the last Americans to make it out when Saigon fell to the North Vietnamese in 1975.

What did he do there? "I did all kinds of things. A minor part of my time there was as an advisor at MACV (pronounced MAC-v, for Military Assistance Command Vietnam). Most of the time I was in the field with combat units, coordinating information. I was caught in combat three times."

In those years military commanders had little regard for field intelligence, even though the information was solid, so his primary frustration was "how often I was not believed. I would tell military commanders that they were about to be attacked and they didn't believe me or I would tell them that the enemy is right over the hill. I know where he is. Go get him. And they didn't believe me. I finally coined a term for that called the Cassandra effect because it happened so often." Cassandra is a character from Greek mythology who had the gift of prophesy but was not believed because she was cursed by Apollo.

The Cassandra effect cost American lives.

"1967. I told the commander of the 4th Infantry Division that the North Vietnamese were getting ready to attack his battalions but he didn't believe me. One was attacked and virtually destroyed and that led to one of the biggest battles of the war. It happened again in the fall of Saigon when I told the ambassador that Saigon was going to be attacked and he didn't believe me." The city fell.

The war ended. Tom made it home with a serious case of what he calls Post Traumatic Stress Injury. He doesn't like the word "disorder." He reported to Ft. Meade and NSA headquarters.

"The war was so unpopular when I got back that no one in the NSA wanted to talk about it. It was dirty and disgraceful. I didn't talk about it, even within the building." He couldn't tell anyone outside the agency that he had even been to Vietnam. He was left to deal with his ghosts by himself. In those years the NSA had therapists to hear stories from employees who had suffered through traumatic events, but there was no future for them there. They lost their clearances. So Tom was left in the desert. Years went by, attitudes changed, the NSA eventually granted Tom a prestigious award for his service during the unpopular war.

He can't talk about his work during the years that followed. He will say that there were times when, as he puts it, "We captured some material that had to be translated immediately and I was there for twenty-eight hours straight."

Working in a spy agency is not like working for IBM or a trucking company, not that smart people are not working at those jobs. Aside from limits on what can be said at home, NSA employees tend to be unusually bright. "The intelligence quotient was very high. People were brilliant. I loved being around them. They were mostly devoted to their work. They came in early and stayed late. It was intriguing, it was fascinating, it was fulfilling. That made it such a pleasure to go to work every day."

Well, most days. “I was once punished for being on the intelligence staff and writing a report critical of NSA. And the director of operations was so angry with me that he assigned me to a room with no responsibility and no job. Nothing. An office that had a window that looked out on the hall and people would walk by and see me at my desk with nothing to do. The window had a curtain on the outside. So I went outside and drew the curtain. And, of course, the next person who walked by opened the curtain again so everybody could walk by and laugh at me.” The operations director moved to a new job and so did Tom. His time as a display lasted about two months.

Tom has no sympathy for people who think the NSA has nothing better to do than spy on American citizens. First, he has no problem with the privacy issue. “I have a lack of understanding when it comes to privacy. There’s nothing in my life that I would hide. But let’s take the issue of privacy. People at NSA are not the least interested in anybody’s private life. They are interested in terrorists, for example. Or people who are going to do harm to the United States. And the whole purpose of looking through these communications is to look for these people and to catch them before they blow up a building or shoot people.”

He says that these very smart people working long days sifting through bits of information for long periods of time know what they’re looking for and they do their jobs well. “The results, of course, are classified. We don’t know what works and what doesn’t but I would be willing to bet my life savings that it has happened repeatedly that we have uncovered plots and stopped them through scanning through all kinds of communications, including those that ordinary people use. How can people object to that? It’s saving their lives, for heaven’s sake.”

After decades in the dark world of intelligence, where small bits are gathered and sifted, where patterns emerge, where lives are saved or lost, Tom has little patience with people who, in his opinion, don't understand how it works.

These days Tom is a writer. He retired as early as he could so he could pursue a fulltime career as an author. "It is the hardest work I've ever done. In the intelligence business there are rules. You know that X follows Y, for example. In writing, that's not true. It is a far more difficult task than intelligence ever was."

How long does it take him to write a book? "About fifteen years. It's the whole process."

That, in its way, is exactly like intelligence work.

(Tom Glenn's books are available at his author page on Amazon.com.)

Eleven

A Life in Medicine

"I was infected with a desire to be a scientist as well as a physician."
Jared Grantham

It's a long way from the wheat fields of western Kansas to the highest honors in medicine. A kid whose early years were spent carrying chamber pots down from the family apartment over the furniture store could not, in conventional thinking, dream of being feted by the best minds in nephrology and honored for ground-breaking research. But that is exactly the journey Jared Grantham took.

Until age fourteen Jared dreamed of playing quarterback for the University of Kansas or pitching for the Yankees. Polio squelched that dream, but the small town doctor who diagnosed the disease helped put Jared on the path that would define his life.

The doctor's name was Ross Field. He was beloved in Johnson. He was called to the Grantham house to look in on Jared, who had taken ill and was in his bed on the second floor of the family's small home at the edge of town. He performed a spinal tap on the boy and the diagnosis was polio. Dr. Field arranged for Jared to be taken to a hospital in Wichita, where he would remain for ten weeks.

Jared Grantham as a boy in Johnson, Kansas

As he lay in bed, he watched the doctors who cared for him. "The physicians who took care of me were surgeons, orthopedic surgeons. The older ones were pretty imperial. They believed they were saints and you had to look at them that way. The younger surgeons were more cordial and would joke with you and make you feel like you were not just a piece of meat, that you were somebody." The experience helped shape his treatment of his own patients in later years.

Back home in Johnson, Jared's life was upside down. No more football. No more baseball. Dr. Field took the boy under his wing. "He felt sorry for me that my life had been wrecked by polio. My best friend had died in an iron lung that spring after we both went into the hospital."

Dr. Field knew that Jared could have a great future. He hired Jared to do menial work around his office and introduced him to medical science. "He would take time showing me things in his laboratory. He dissected some testicles out of a grasshopper. He made a smash preparation on the slide and I could see the sperm swimming around. It was really impressive for a young man. I was a high school sophomore at the time. I decided I wanted to go into medicine."

Dr. Field was killed in an accident before Jared graduated from high school. The entire town mourned and Jared mourned as deeply as anyone. Dr. Field was a model for the physician Jared wanted to be.

"I also got a taste for the kind of doctor I didn't want to be. When I was a senior in high school I developed a very high white blood cell count and I turned jaundiced. My urine was bright orange. I was urinating bile." With Dr. Field gone, Jared had to visit a physician in nearby Ulysses, Kansas. "He was kind of a callous guy," Jared says. The doctor told Jared he had a high white blood cell count. Jared knew enough science to know what it could possibly mean. Leukemia. "Yes, it could be," the doctor said. Jared was devastated and spent an agonizing twenty-four hours waiting for the test results, thinking the worst. "So here I was with leukemia. I had had polio. It was just awful."

The next day the physician told him he had infectious mononucleosis, not leukemia. Jared vowed that he would never leave a patient to worry needlessly and give them anguished moments without a firm diagnosis.

He did well at the University of Kansas Medical School and even published three papers from research he helped conduct with faculty. He graduated with top grades and completed a two-year residency before he was accepted to a program at the National Institutes of Health in Bethesda, Maryland, where he joined the leading kidney research team in the world.

He spent five years at NIH, a time of professional and personal growth. He worked with some of the finest minds in medicine. What did he learn in those years?

Jared Grantham, young physician/scientist

“I learned about myself. I learned that I was creative. I learned that I could survive in difficult situations. I learned that there were a hell of a lot more smart people out there than me. You benefit from being around smart people. If you want to be successful you need to be with people who are smarter than you. Is also conditioned me for becoming a leader and knowing that when I started hiring people I should hire people smarter than I am.”

Fast forward a few decades and Jared is acknowledged as one of the world's leading kidney researchers. His work has had a major impact on the understanding and treatment of polycystic kidney disease and could potentially improve the lives of tens of thousands of people who suffer from it.

The kid from far western Kansas had arrived. He was honored by the world's leading researchers and was feted in far-away foreign cities.

"It was exciting to feel appreciated that what you were doing was passing muster with the greatest minds in nephrology. I was always fighting the arrogance factor." His philosophy is to not call attention to himself, to be "discovered," as he puts it. "Consequently, I only get accolades if I deserve them. I'm not getting any political payoffs or popularity contests. Anything I've gotten through the years has been earned. I have never been given something I didn't earn."

Now, as eighty nears, does he reflect on his life and his good fortune to have a distinguished career in his chosen field and a fine family?

"Lord, yes, all the time at this stage of my life. I spend a lot of time thinking about things. I've had an effective partner for fifty-seven years. If I hadn't found Carol as a sophomore at Baker University, I really doubt I would have accomplished as much as I have."

There will be more about the impact of Carol on Jared's life in chapter 16 as we look at the impact of women on these seven men.

Twelve

Life as a Soldier

"I am the Infantry.
I am my country's strength in War,
her deterrent in peace.
I am the heart of the fight –
wherever, whenever."
Infantryman's Creed

"The whole thing about the decorations
is we've been there, we've done that,
and we can continue the march."
Grady Smith

Full disclosure: I grew up around soldiers. When I was a boy nearly every man I knew had been in combat in World War Two, including my father. I listened to stories of battles and rifles and courage. I have a special place in my heart for those who have lived in the mud, known extreme fear and tremble in their dreams. The infantry is the pride of the Army, even though many soldiers would disagree and pray that they are never assigned to an infantry unit. The life is hard. Even the training is dangerous. But when conflict comes it is the infantry that gets the job done. Infantry is boots on the ground. They're called ground pounders for good reason. Their insignia is crossed rifles, muskets in honor of the Minutemen, from whom they are descended. George Washington is forever their first commander. Not everyone is cut out for the infantry. Some seek it.

One of those men is Grady Smith. As a young man he studied to be a priest, decided that celibacy was not for him, and pursued a love of theatre. But as young men often discover, his road was not straight and he dropped out of a PhD program and enlisted in the Army under a contract that would send him to Officers Candidate School after Basic Training. This was in 1964 and the Vietnam War was building and the Army needed infantry officers. Grady "tabbed up" to use an old expression. After he was commissioned he went to Ranger School, Jungle Warfare School, Airborne School. He joined the famed 82nd Airborne Division as a platoon leader and spent time on a clean-up operation in the Dominican Republic after the United States had intervened to prevent a communist takeover.

But the gods of war were waiting. Vietnam was absorbing as many infantryman as the United States could provide and by 1968 Grady was company commander of a rifle company in war.

His hearing, never optimal, took a beating in the noise of training and combat. In an age before earplugs, soldiers accepted that their ears would ring and some loss would occur. Rifle rounds, artillery explosions, hand grenades and other tools of combat make a lot of noise. Finally, Grady had to be medevaced out. He couldn't hear much out of one ear and was losing his hearing in the other. But not before he had been awarded a Silver Star, Combat Infantry Badge, and other decorations for valor and leadership in combat.

"I was going to adios the Army when I got back from Vietnam. I was medevaced for ear surgery at Scott Air Force Base in Illinois. Then I went to Ft. Leonard Wood in Missouri for out-processing. I taught English at a local school. I was applying to get back into grad school to work on a doctorate in theatre." The applications were submitted and he waited for an acceptance letter someplace, anyplace. "I always seemed to wind up on the list of people they were considering but not high enough to get in."

He talked it over with his wife. "I signed back on to active duty. I was assigned to Ft. Benning." Not long after he signed on with the Army, he received a letter from the University of Minnesota accepting him for a graduate position. It was too late.

"I was a captain. I went to Ft. Benning with a master's degree in theater and I'm not sure it was cross relevant to anything that crossed rifle people do but there was a shortage of master's degrees and they put me as an instructor on how to teach." Crossed rifles are the infantry insignia. It's a safe bet that theater is not taught in advanced infantry training. "After that I was reassigned at the advanced infantry officer course, the one that teaches you how to be a staff officer."

With his combat experience and training, the Green Berets came calling and he received orders to join Special Forces. "Somebody finally looked at my personnel file and saw that I wore a hearing aid. You can't jump into a 130 mph prop blast from a C-130 with a hearing aid," he says, laughing. The Green Berets lost their man.

Grady's wife, Katy, is of German ancestry, so he applied to the Defense Language Institute, formerly the Army Language School, to learn German. A year later Grady was assigned to a post in Germany, helping American servicemen and women find housing off base. He was then assigned to an equal employment opportunity office to ensure that the troops were not subject to discrimination. He and his family spent three-and-a-half-years in Germany, enjoying the culture and the food.

An assignment as an EEO officer in Illinois was followed by acceptance to the Command and General Staff College at Ft. Leavenworth, Kansas, a course for officers whom the Army feels are going places. He next went to the headquarters of Army's Adjutant General in Washington as a staff officer. A great assignment for an officer whose infantry days were behind him.

But combat never really leaves the mind or the soul. It haunted Grady. In Washington he joined a creative writing group to help him get his mind off what he had seen and done. He enrolled in George Mason University to resume his education.

But his infantry past was always there, always a kind of mini biography on his chest. Ribbons signifying distinguished service and bravery under fire. The Ranger tab. The jump wings. The patch on his right shoulder that told the world he had been in combat and with which unit.

"I could go from Europe to the United States, from Vietnam to Ft. Benning. I could go to Ft. Sheridan and put my suitcase down and my competence was assumed. I didn't have to prove anything to anybody."

He didn't have to prove anything to himself, either. "The stuff on your chest runs two ways. It shows the people who look at you who you are and it reminds you who you are and the fact that you are competent. It is demonstrated competence at a high level."

He retired as a Lieutenant Colonel with twenty years of service to his country. He retired to teach.

Thirteen

In Search of Fairness

I could actually say I helped people.
I made a difference.
Lamont Gibson

It is the rare man who spends his life doing the work that rights the wrongs he experienced as a boy and a young man. Lamont Gibson is such a man. Earlier in the book he talked about the discrimination he experienced growing up, the unfairness and the racism.

Air Force Lt. Colonel Lamont Gibson with General Richard Myers, Chairman of the Joint Chiefs of Staff

Lamont wore many hats during his working life. He was a reserve Air Force officer and he worked in intelligence for the federal government. But his primary work was ensuring that hiring practices at federal agencies was fair. He worked in equal employment opportunity.

"I was director of EEO for the National Credit Union Administration. I was Director of EEO for the Defense Information Systems Agency when they were the Defense Communications Agency. I was Deputy Director for EEO at the U. S. Department of Housing and Urban Development for complaint processing. I looked into all of the complaints that were filed against managers at the Department of Housing and Urban Development. I was Branch Chief in charge of complaint processing policy for the Department of the Navy. I worked for Clarence Thomas when he first took the job as Chairman of the Equal Employment Opportunity Commission. I was his Chief of Affirmative Action."

Lamont makes clear that he did not see his work as racial score-settling or a way to give white people a taste of their own medicine, even if those white people held unkind thoughts about people of color. "It was a responsibility to do the right thing, to not trample on the rights of the alleged discriminator because I personally felt that they were that type of person. You don't trample on the rights of a person because you don't like them." He adds that he didn't favor those he did like, even those who brought complaints of discrimination. "The work comes in finding the truth."

The 1964 Civil Rights Act applied to the entire nation. It made it illegal to discriminate on the basis of race, color, religion, sex, or national origin. It ended unfair voting practices and made it illegal for hotels and other public accommodations to restrict their services to certain classes of people. It was landmark legislation that is credited with changing the American social structure.

Only it did not apply to the federal government. That didn't happen until 1972. The intervening years gave federal government managers a lower standard of fairness than the rest of America. They could discriminate against anyone. They did not have to offer a valid reason for not hiring someone, or firing someone. The federal management system was dominated by white men who tended to favor other white men. "It was accepted to call blacks niggers. It was accepted to say 'Get your ass out of here. I'm firing you' for little or no reason," he says.

After the Civil Rights Act was extended to the federal government things changed. During the 1970s men and women like Lamont ran training sessions for federal employees to explain what injustice is. "People have been trained in what not to say or what to do. Military officers have been sent to schools and taught how to act. So when you talk to a person about what happened there is a reality setting in. They know what really happened. They also know what their reaction should have been."

Training in fairness was only part of the job for Lamont. Processing complaints was the other part. This is where his own sense of fairness came into play. "To some degree it was walking a thin line. I could not represent the people. I could not represent the agency. I had to stand in the middle and look to see if the person had a case. Would a reasonable-minded person believe they may have been discriminated against? Once you establish a case you have to weigh the evidence, and then the work comes in finding the evidence. People don't take notes. They don't write the day and time with these witnesses. Too often a person who allegedly did something will say 'I didn't do it' or 'It didn't happen.'"

Lamont's challenge was to be credible. He knew he had to be listened to, to be taken seriously. "When I talked to people, I knew that the color of my skin made a difference. So how I presented myself was important. How I dressed. How I stood. Did I know the Queen's English? If they could have taken me lightly they would have. You have to command respect when they see you, before you speak, and when you speak they have to know you are a force to be reckoned with."

He reported to agency heads, not a remote committee or office. At the Quantico Marine Base he reported to a three-star general. "When I spoke people would listen because I had the ear of the head of the agency."

Through the 70s and 80s and into the 90s things began to change. Attitudes changed. "The way you change people's attitudes is through training, constant training. When I grew up you had to be better than a white person to be considered equal to them. Nowadays people are not looking at your skin color. They are looking at your performance." Or, as Dr. Martin Luther King put it, they are not looking at the color of your skin, but the content of your character. His dream, expressed in 1963, is a reality for millions of Americans.

Lamont is retired now and enjoying his life. He lives comfortably and has the satisfaction of knowing that part of the change in America over these past fifty years has been because of him and people like him. The humiliation people of color suffered as part of their daily lives when he was a boy is no longer tolerated by society in general. Many federal agency heads are people of color. Many are women. Others are gay. Most Americans now know what discrimination is. They know what it means to do the right thing.

What would Lamont say to a young person who wants to follow in his tracks? "You have to want to be there because it's more than just a job. You have to be passionate about it to help people. You have to stand on the side of justice."

When we as Americans congratulate ourselves about how far we've come in race, gender and other issues, we can thank people like Lamont who showed us how to be fair to each other.

Fourteen

The Detective

"The majority of police officers are good people trying to do a good job."
Jim King

There are more than one million full and part-time law enforcement officers in the United States. About 765,000 of them have arrest powers. In 2012 alone there were one and a quarter-million violent crimes and many more millions of other types of crimes. There are more crimes than cops. I will stay away from the debate about the criminal justice system and whether it is fair and whether too many activities are against the law. The fact is, we need police. If a burglar were coming through your window who would you call?

Police work is public service. Those who spend their lives in such work are making society better by keeping the rest of us out of the clutches of violent sociopaths, con artists, and other folks who make up the dark matter of society.

So how does someone become a cop? Jim King was lured into it by a program to bring more college educated men and women onto the police force in Montgomery County, Maryland, a suburb of Washington, D.C. "I had more than enough hours to graduate but they weren't the right hours. I had changed majors many times."

For college guys like Jim, the county offered to bring professors to the police stations and pay for the courses. And if the new student/officers had sixty hours of credits, the county added ten per cent to their pay. When they graduated the bonus went up to fifteen per cent. Jim signed up at for a starting salary of $7,005 per year. "I said, hey, I like this." It was 1968.

He was assigned as a patrol officer in Bethesda, a wealthy area that abuts Northwest Washington, also a wealthy area. "There were complaints about barking dogs and neighbor problems," he said. Bethesda is home to people who feel they are entitled. Members of Congress, for example. "I would take a report about a neighbor's trash blowing across the yard."

There were occasional robberies and even murders, but mostly it was minor stuff and traffic accidents. "I enjoyed investigating those because you had to use your brain to reconstruct accidents and testify in court. It was one of the few things you could investigate from beginning to end and nobody took it away from you." Other, bigger crimes were handed over to detectives.

He didn't like writing tickets, thinking it was bad public relations for the department. He gave out warnings, often to people who didn't have the money pay a ticket. "But they kept me on because I was a hell of an accident investigator."

Detective Jim King

He saw a notice about an opening for detective and sent in a letter of interest. He was accepted and was assigned to the youth division in Wheaton, a not-so-wealthy suburb. This was in the 70s when the youth culture at the time created teenage runaways, boys and girls, who left home for life somewhere, anywhere, else. "We would take a report from parents and go looking for them."

Some kids would get caught shoplifting and Jim and his partners would lecture them about the perils of a life of crime. "It worked in general. Sometimes it didn't."

In the late 70s homes in expensive neighborhoods began reporting burglaries in which only high-end items were taken, things such rare paintings and antiques. It happened in Bethesda and Potomac in Montgomery County, the tony Chevy Chase section of D.C., Fairfax county in Virginia and other areas where wealthy people enjoyed big homes and high-dollar furnishings.

Jim had developed an interest in antiques through his contact with jewelers and antique stores in Bethesda, stores that had reported robberies. He went to shows and borrowed books from store owners. "I could tell the difference between an oriental rug and an oil painting," he jokes. "That made me an expert in the police department."

He began to investigate the high-end burglaries. He met with other detectives from the jurisdictions around Washington and saw a pattern. The burglar, whoever he was, worked during the winter months when daylight was short and worked in the evening, generally while the people who lived in the expensive homes were out. There were similar burglaries in Richmond, Virginia.

"I started putting two and two together and thought, it's the same guy. This guy was very active, hitting four or five houses a night."

He learned of a man who had escaped from a prison in upstate New York. His name was Bernard Welch. "I ran across a rape victim who had been raped when this guy went to her house to rob it. When he raped her he kissed her and she felt his teeth move. He had false teeth." He wrote to the prison and asked if they had dental records on this fellow named Bernard Welch and if so, did he have false teeth. The answer was yes and yes. "That clinched it. I knew he was in the Washington area and he was stealing art and antiques. I didn't know where he was, what name he was using or where he was selling it. I wrote to auction houses up and down the East Coast and sent a kind of wanted poster with his picture and what he might be selling. I never got a response."

Welch had a common-law wife who was from Duluth, Minnesota. During the winter months he broke into houses and stole items worth a fortune. During the summer months he was in Minnesota selling these items.

It came to an end when Welch broke into the home of a prominent Washington area surgeon named Dr. Michael Halberstam. It was 1980. Dr. Halberstam and his wife had gone out and returned home early. Welch was on the second floor. The Halberstams were on the first floor. He was trapped. "He tried to sneak out. There was a fight downstairs. Welch drew down with a gun and ran out the door. The doctor chased him and there was a scuffle in the yard. Welch unloaded five shots, missed three times, and hit the doctor twice, once in the chest and once in the side."

Dr. Halberstam fell as Welch ran away but he managed to get to his feet, thinking that he had not been seriously wounded. He and his wife jumped into their car and set out for a nearby hospital. On the way they saw Welch running through someone's yard and the doctor drove up over the curb and ran over Welch. He kept going but before he got to the hospital he passed out from loss of blood and his car hit a tree. He was taken to the hospital but died on the operating table.

Neighbors who heard the commotion called police and Welch was found under a bush with the gun and items stolen from the Halberstam home. D.C. police contacted Jim King who identified Welch. The Ghost Burglar's time in the Washington area was over.

How much did he steal? "I can only talk about the five years he was here. He robbed between three- and five-thousand houses. He only picked the best neighborhoods and stole the best things. He had a fine eye. Somewhere between $50 and $100 million."

There is a postscript to the story. Welch escaped from an "escape proof" jail in Chicago and was later captured in

Pittsburgh on a routine traffic stop. He died in prison. Jim King wrote about the case in his book *The Ghost Burglar.*

Did he find detective work satisfying? "I did. I always liked puzzles."

Do TV detective shows come close to reality? "No, not really."

"Police work is ninety per cent boredom and ten per cent terror. You go many days without doing anything exciting. Then you have ten minutes of terror as you are chasing someone or being shot at. It's not for the faint of heart."

Is it a good career for a young person? "Yes, very rewarding. You get to see the dark underbelly of society. It's a reality check."

Fifteen

Boss Jock

"Johnny Holliday is not only a talented broadcaster, actor, and athlete, but an outstanding coach. I know because he was my coach in both baseball and basketball. Of course he organized both teams and made himself the coach."
Sal Bando, World Champion Oakland Athletics

John Holliday Bobbitt, the kid from Miami who worked odd jobs out of high school, rode the crest of what was known at Top 40 radio as one of the country's top disc jockeys. In 1965 he was named *the* top jock. You can experience some of his radio work at the Rock and Roll Hall of Fame in Cleveland, where he ruled the airwaves in the 60s.

How did it happen? How did the kid from south Florida find himself at the top of rock radio when rock radio was at the top of the entire culture – and then move into the top ranks of sportscasters?

Earlier chapters detailed his early years in Perry, Georgia, and Rochester, New York, where he learned the DJ craft. This story will begin in Cleveland, where he made the leap to the top. He got an offer from Metromedia, a big broadcast company at the time, to join the staff at WHK.

"When I went to Cleveland we went with the idea that we had no place to go but up. They were last in the ratings. They were playing wall to wall all over the place with music with no real identifiable personalities. It had no direction and no excitement. It was the perfect situation." Metromedia fired the entire staff and brought in a new team, all in their twenties, Johnny included.

"I was twenty-one at the time. They put a new sound on. They had new jingles. They put echo on the station. They had news a fifty-five. All sorts of things to ramp it up and make it more exciting. We kind of took the city by storm. In six months we knocked off KYW." KYW had been Cleveland's number one station. "We were solid number one in all dayparts."

At one point Johnny's numbers in the afternoon drive-time slot were so high that he had more listeners than every other station in the city combined. The evening man's ratings were even higher. "We were darn good," he says, "we had it all going for us." Johnny was a top jock for the princely sum of $160 a week to start. Five years later, having won the market, he was making $225.

Those were the days of high school sock hops and personal appearances by the music stars whom the kids liked. It was the early 60s, rock's heyday. The radio business was competitive and if a station group wanted a personality out of a certain market, they lured him to a bigger market.

WHK's owners, Metromedia, hired a competitor in Cleveland and put him on the air in New York. Westinghouse Broadcasting responded by hiring Johnny away from WHK and making him the afternoon jock at WINS in New York. After five years in Cleveland, Johnny found himself on the same station with the legendary Murray the K, who ruled New York evenings. He made three times what he made in Cleveland, plus generous talent fees. "Here I am in New

York, twenty-six years old, making more money than I thought was possible."

A year and a half later WINS dropped the rock format and went all-news. The Boss Jocks, all of them, were out of work. For Johnny, it wasn't for long. A man named Clint Churchill, who had tried to hire him years earlier, had purchased KYA in San Francisco and turned it into a rocker. He wanted Johnny to be his morning man.

Johnny Holliday with the Four Seasons,
a popular rock group, in San Francisco

It was a natural fit. He had the freedom to do whatever he wanted in his off hours. He organized the Radio Oneders basketball and softball teams that played for charities. He got major Bay Area sports stars to play on the teams. Stars like Sal Bando of the Athletics and Rick Barry of the Warriors. The teams raised large sums of money by drawing big crowds.

Johnny's ratings were strong. He was in demand. He was the announcer on NBC Television's variety shows Hullabaloo and the Roger Miller Show. He was named America's Number One Disc Jockey in 1965. He co-hosted the Beatles' final concert in Candlestick Park.

He was on top of the world. But he was also restless. He was tired of rock radio's strict format. Play the hits, over and over, keep it moving, don't talk too much. He considered getting out of the music radio business and going over to sports full time.

By then, KYA had been sold to Avco Broadcasting. He told them he wanted something more than the rock format. "Avco owned a station in Washington, WWDC. Middle of the road format. The station had the Senators, the Bullets, Navy football. They said you can do the morning show. You can do personality, whatever you want to do."

So in 1969 Johnny moved his family one last time. He took over the morning show at WWDC and let his talent loose. He worked hard. He allowed his newscasters to do characters on his show. He let the sports guy do shtick. He prerecorded bits and skits. He turned the traffic reporter, the storied "Captain" Dan Rosenson, into a character who once sang Happy Birthday to a listener after Johnny convinced him that the rest of the staff was also going to sing. Captain Dan could not hear the station when he was broadcasting over his two-way radio, so he had no idea that he was singing alone in the skies over Washington. Johnny's only contribution to the song was hysterical laughter at Dan's terrible voice. Johnny did dinner theater. He did sports. He was everywhere. As he had in Rochester, Cleveland, New York and San Francisco, he became a fixture in the city. He was everybody's favorite, whether popular music guy, sports guy, dinner theater singer and dancer, he was the man.

By 1978 Johnny was finished with radio music. After more than twenty years of playing the hits he was ready to do something else. The station that had been the ratings leader for decades in Washington was WMAL, a so-called full-service station with an established morning team of Harden and Weaver, ratings leaders among adults for as long as anyone could remember. WMAL carried the Redskins, far-and-away the most popular team in the market. The station carried University of Maryland football and basketball.

"I was hired by WMAL to go over there and eventually, when Harden and Weaver retired, I was going to slip into that. I did sports for them. I was able to do dinner theater. I did sports on ABC." ABC owned WMAL at the time. "I was waiting for Harden and Weaver to retire. They never did."

It didn't matter. Johnny became an established sports personality in the Washington area. He has been with the University of Maryland for nearly four decades.

So now, in his 79th year, after all those radio stations, all that success and acclaim, all the fame and the play-by-play, the accolades and friendships with rock stars and famous athletes, what has it been like to be Johnny Holliday?

"It's been phenomenal."

Part Six

The Women in Their Lives

Wives are young men's mistresses, companions for middle age, and old men's nurses.

Francis Bacon

Sixteen

I wouldn't be where I am today without her.
Jared Grantham

"Who were the most important women in your life?"

Most of these men said, "My mother." Then came wives. Some had more than one.

Let's begin with Jared Grantham, the world-renowned medical researcher. His mother's name was Ista, a name whose origins are unknown. Family lore has it that her mother made it up. Her maiden name was Taylor. Her married name was Grantham. She was a woman of strong opinions which she was not reluctant to share.

"She was very protective. In my book (*Why I Think About Urine*) I call her a lioness ready to swat away anything that threatened her cub," Jared says. "She had great dreams for me. She entered me in a perfect baby contest in Dodge City and she was upset that I didn't win."

Ista adored her only son. "It was a relationship I took advantage of. I was a momma's boy for many years. I took piano lessons and violin lessons. I didn't particularly enjoy it because I wanted to be outside. She always pushed me."

In his sophomore year at Baker University in eastern Kansas, Jared fell in love. It was the first and last time. The love affair has lasted sixty years.

Jared's physical limitations had eroded his self-confidence around young women. "I had a dim perception of myself as a masculine presence that would be attractive to women. I saw my body as something put together with discarded parts."

He sang in the Baker choir. For a year he watched a young women whom he assumed would never give him the time of day. "She was one of those untouchables. She could never be interested in me."

In the spring he complained to his accompanist that he didn't have a date to the prom. His accompanist said her roommate didn't have a date, either, and maybe he should think about asking her. He finally gathered his courage and she said yes. Her name was Carol.

"We had a good time. We went to a formal dance. She was kind of exotic. She was very quiet and reserved. She'd grown up on a farm. She had a reputation among my fraternity brothers as the Baldwin Icebox."

There was a second date. And a third. "On our third date I worked up my courage to kiss her goodbye at the sorority house. I was smitten. Bells were ringing. Electricity was up and down my spine. It was like that for the rest of my time at Baker."

They graduated in May of 1958. They were married in June. That summer they lived with Jared's parents in Johnson, Kansas. The newlyweds slept upstairs in a very small house. It was not an ideal situation for a newly married couple. That fall Jared began medical school at the University of Kansas in Lawrence. Carol got a job teaching thirty-five miles away in Kansas City. He walked to class and she drove winding roads in the early hours. In those years medical students were in Lawrence for their first year and at the KU Medical Center in Kansas City for years two through four.

Carol's job netted the couple $250 a month to live on. She became pregnant when Jared was a fourth year student and had to leave teaching. That fall his intern pay was $150 a month. There were three of them now. "We lived out of the dented cans section of the grocery store." A year later his residency brought the family's income to $200 a month.

Carol kept the family going by taking care of their daughter, managing what little money they had, and keeping house. Jared's star was rising. He was accepted to a position at the National Institutes of Health at the princely sum of $833.33 per month. "We were in hog heaven."

It was during those years that Jared became hard to live with. "I was kind of impressed with myself," he says. "I was continuously moving ahead and Carol was changing diapers and trying to figure out how to make the money go." He was arrogant and suggested that she expand her mind, oblivious to the challenges she faced caring a growing family. It finally occurred to him that he was being unfair. In fact, Carol was holding it all together.

Now, years later, after he has distinguished himself and been feted all over the world for his groundbreaking research, he knows who got him there.

What has Carol meant to him?

"Everything. I wouldn't be where I am today without her. No way. I can't think of many women who would have tolerated me during my nasty years and helped me accomplish as much as I have. Without her I couldn't have done it."

Time and experience have given him an appreciation of the young woman who had him hearing bells back at Baker University. He sees her as his intellectual equal. "She is a very wise woman. She makes good fundamental decisions. If I have something I'm concerned about I go to her to help me resolve it."

Time has also blended them together. "We do think alike on lots of things. We find ourselves thinking the same thoughts out of the blue. We both enjoy doing the same things."

As we saw in an earlier chapter, Jared writes poems. In 1992 he wrote one to Carol. It was during a period in which he was receiving many awards for his medical research. In his acceptance speeches he credits her with his success. He expressed it in the poem.

Awards rained down,
Accolades for heavy deeds.
"A power in his field!"
How does one of common stock
Achieve such things?
Despite physical weaknesses
That would give excuse for failure?
Look to the soul mate.
The one whose love and commitment
Energize his half-body
She's his body armor.
A presence bringing confidence
That genes neglected.
Look beside him for the soul battery
That lifts him above the ken.

Seventeen

My mother was an alcoholic. She did the best she could but it wasn't very good.
Tom Glenn

Not every man has a Carol in his life. Many men get off to a rocky start and take time to come to peace with the opposite sex. Most of the men in these stories list their mothers as the primary female relationship in their lives, followed by wives. Tom listed his mother last. In fact, he needed prodding to discuss her.

"My parents are not people I remember happily." His father, as you read earlier, was in and out of prison and died in a bar fight. His mother drank. "I have a memory from my childhood of being locked in a car while they (his parents) were in a bar drinking. I managed to get out of the car and went from bar to bar looking for them. I remember being very severely punished for having interrupted them. It was a very bad childhood. They were terrible parents. I don't talk about them."

Tom was estranged from his mother for many years but arranged to see her the day before she died. He never reconciled with his father. He is not one who will outline how he was shaped by his mother and he will not join the others in their feelings that "mom" was there for him when he was a boy.

So, who are the most important women in his life? He is not using their names.

“The women I have been married to or lived with. There have been four of them.”

Let’s begin with wife number one.

“The woman I married first, who was the mother of my children. She died about three years ago. She and I were divorced, oh Lord, thirty years ago or something. A long time ago.”

It was an NSA love story. They both spoke Vietnamese and French. He was in the Army at the time and worked as a civilian linguist. “We gravitated toward each other,” he says. What attracted him to her? “I found her very touching, unsure of herself. She felt like she was an outlier. She was not particularly attractive as a woman. I found out over time that her principal emotion was fear. It was the fact that she was so willing to depend on me that attracted me. I was touched by her. She asked me to marry her. A woman in tears can move me to do things that I should know better than to do.” It was not a shotgun wedding. They refrained from intimacy of that sort until they were married. “It was a bad marriage from the beginning. She was an extremely poor mother. I said I can’t live this way any longer. It lasted twenty years.”

He met wife number two in the group Parents Without Partners. “She was a delightful woman. The love of my life. I loved her so much I couldn’t see straight. We lived together for fifteen years or so. Because of our children we decided to get married. That was the death of the relationship. After two years or so she decided she didn’t want to be with me anymore and that was the end of the marriage. She was very strong, very capable, very articulate. A delight from beginning to end.”

Not every man would say that about an ex-wife. He doesn't say that about wife number three. "Something like the first marriage in that I was dating this woman I was not in love with but I felt sorry for her. She broke down in tears and begged me to marry her and I did. I knew it was a mistake. The marriage did not go well at all." It didn't last very long.

He is now in serious relationship number four. It is very different from the others "if for no other reason than the fact that we're both approaching eighty. That makes a big difference in life." He says, "She is a strong, independent woman who stands on her own two feet."

Tom was diagnosed with cancer in 2015 and underwent surgery, chemotherapy and radiation. It made him very sick. She stuck with him and cared for him. It was a very important reminder that people do care and the deprivation of his childhood is over.

Time has given Tom a new sense of purpose in his dealings with the woman in his life. "For the first time in my life I'm taking pleasure in pleasing her, doing things that she likes. She likes flowers so I have lots of flowers around the house. I found out what kinds of foods she likes so I cook them for her. These days she's the light of my life."

It's a nice way to end a story that began on rocky ground with a mother who wasn't "very good," to use his words. He has someone he cares for and who cares for him. His health is shaky and she is there for him. He is at peace with women.

So what has Tom learned about women after all these years and all these relationships?

"That's an interesting question. I don't know the answer to it. I make no pretense of understanding women. At a conscious level, they baffle me."

On the other hand, "They have a profound influence on me and my life and how I understand things. They made me understand nurturing and gentleness, which didn't come naturally to me. My instincts told me to excel and be big and bold and all those things. It took women to teach me that nurturing is as much a male instinct as dominating is. I learned a lot from them."

Eighteen

I proposed on our second date
Grady Smith

Who was the most important woman in your life?

The question was posed to Grady Smith, the retired Army officer, combat veteran, theater scholar, and PhD.

"It comes in two shifts," he said. "My mom as I was growing up. As life went on Katy took over that role." Katy is his wife of forty-nine years.

Mom is almost always the most important woman in anyone's early life. Men of the generation we're talking to had fathers who were, by the standards of today, distant and uninvolved.

"Dad would come home from work, get the paper and wait for dinner," Grady says. Many if not most dads of that era were like that. We're talking about the forties and fifties.

Grady's mother was named Marie. She was the oldest of eight children. As a girl she showed a talent for painting and was offered a scholarship to a prestigious high school in St. Louis. Her father said no. Marie, at age fourteen, went to work in a hat factory, not an unusual story for kids of the early twentieth century.

Marie introduced Grady to the arts, first painting, then guitar and finally children's theater. He was hooked. She took him to museums and other centers of art. But her lessons were about more than art. "She taught me hard work and discipline, which I still struggle to grab." Marie was the disciplinarian, the parent who issued a swat across Grady's butt on occasion.

When he went off to college he didn't go to a co-educational institution where the boys and girls did what young people have done since the dawn of time, learning the mating game. He went to a seminary where he studied to be a priest, a "celibate priest," as he puts it. Celibacy was not for him and he left the seminary when he was twenty-two and "in a positive fever to catch up to where I thought my contemporaries were on the lady side." Translation: he was looking for some action. He admits he was a bit obvious about his intentions and the young ladies he encountered knew it. His average was very low. "Did I ring the bell that often? No, I certainly did not."

As a graduate student in Iowa he was teaching a class and, to use his phrase, the bell rang. "This young lady was one of my students. I got her pregnant and we got married because we wanted to do the right thing. It was exactly the wrong thing. I was too immature to carry out my part of the marriage contract." Divorce proceedings were begun before the baby was delivered. The infant, a girl, was placed for adoption and grew up with a family in Atlanta. Years later, after the child was a grown woman, they connected and are now in a loving relationship.

In the summer of 1964, as Grady was preparing to join the Army, he was working in summer stock in St. Louis. A young woman came by the theater after the evening shift where she worked. Her name was Katy.

Was it love at first sight? "Pretty close. I proposed on our second date." Grady knew he was going into the infantry and that meant a combat tour in Vietnam. "When you go into a combat arm like the infantry and you're going to a combat tour and you've got a lady who's returning your vibrations you go for the brass ring. I was really lucky."

Katy became an Army wife, following Grady to one assignment after another. Germany, stateside posts, and the normal family upheaval of career soldiers. "It can be very trying and it was for both of us. It's a very complex weave, the (marital) underlayment."

So now, after nearly five decades together, what has she meant to him? "Oh my goodness. She's a leveling agent. Sometimes I get weird shit in my head. She keeps me from acting on them. Sometimes she doesn't and I pay the consequences." They, like many long-time couples, like the same things. "We share many cultural interests, political interests. She was raised Catholic, too. We say the marriage has lasted so long because we're in a three-story townhouse. My office is on the first floor and hers is on the third, so we never see each other except for lunch."

They spend Sundays together. "We meet in the living room with the *Washington Post* and the *New York Times* and an urn of coffee and we just talk about whatever we want to talk about a news story or an art exhibit review. Anything. We do brunch. In the afternoon we go maybe to the National Gallery or the theater. We have season tickets to five or six different theaters."

Long relationships that stretch over decades develop their own ecologies. Couples know each other's moods and even thoughts. "We can both be pretty stubborn on the things we really want. I think another part of the thread woven into our marriage is knowing when to cave and that's on both sides. You kind of learn what is really important to her or to me and once you pick up on that vibration then it's time to cave."

When we spoke, Katy was pressing him to rent an apartment in New York for a couple of weeks. He was working on a book and needed research time and wanted to stay home. New York it was.

Nineteen

She taught me how to read.
Jim King

Jim King, the former police detective, today is a writer. His book *Ghost Burglar* is about the capture of one of the nation's most notorious burglars. He also writes science fiction. But his love of the written word did not happen early. As a very young boy he had no interest in books or reading of any kind. He didn't know how to read.

When asked about the most important women in his life he mentioned his mother first but he quickly added, "Mrs. Austin. She was my teacher. She taught me how to read." When he transferred from Prince Georges County, Maryland, to Arlington, Virginia, he was eight years old and he could not read, at least not well enough to grasp what was on the paper. "For some reason she took a shine to me, a kid with ADHD, which we didn't have a name for at the time."

She taught him in the third grade and then, the following year, she taught him in the 4th grade. Those two years changed his life. In the fifth grade he was back in Prince Georges County, in what today would be called "affordable housing." His parents were both government workers. "It was all we could afford."

He was back in the school system that had failed to teach him a basic skill. "I was a reader by then and that's what saved me. I started reading everything I could. I was far ahead of everybody else in the class as far as reading was concerned."

His mother, Marguerite, was the family disciplinarian. She and his father married young. She was eighteen, he was twenty.

"My mother was a very loving woman. I was an only child. She was the nurturer." She doled out discipline but she also protected him. "I was an active kid, typical little boy doing stupid stuff. She cleaned it up before my father came home so I wouldn't get in trouble."

She died at age forty-nine from breast cancer.

Jim met Joanna when he was twenty-one and just out of the Navy. "Standard issue Irish Catholic. Tall, pretty, quiet." They dated for three or four years before they were married. "I was going to college and driving a cab. She had a job. We had a little apartment in Silver Spring. We paid $120 a month for it. We were happy. We had friends. We were never ones to go out to nightclubs."

She smoothed his rough edges. He was, he says, "socially inept in the adult world." As we learned in an earlier chapter, they had three children, the first of whom died as a child after a long battle with cancer. They went through it together and became stronger. But this story does not have a happy ending, even though it is a story about profound love. It is a story about two people who made a life together, who endured terrible pain, and then, the end. She died of cancer after forty-one years of marriage.

"If you're married long enough, the two of you become one. Your thoughts always include her and what she would want or what she would expect and her thoughts worked the same way. It's so gradual, this melding of the two of you into one that you don't understand or realize that merging. Only when one dies it's like having a hand cut off. It's such a vacuum. Such a loss. You kind of wander around and bounce off the walls and wonder what to do. You don't have anybody to talk to. There is no *we* anymore."

Three women who shaped him. A teacher who taught him to read, a mother who nurtured him, and a wife who gave him everything.

"Now I have my kids and they hold me together and give me a purpose."

Twenty

We met in fifth grade.
Jim Bohannon

Jim Bohannon was quick to answer the question about the most important women in his life. "There are three," he said. "My mother Dorothy, my first wife Camille and my second wife Annabelle."

Let's begin with mom. "She was quite a remarkable woman. She was a high school graduate. Her family kept her at home as a kind of semi-slave. That's why she didn't graduate until she was 19. She never thought of going to college. I suppose in her own way she was quite liberated. She was a manager for the phone company for a while. She would never have used the word 'liberated'".

Jim grew up as an only child. A brother had died at birth a few years before Jim was born. "After I was born she became an overnight supermom. She looked after me. She helped with bake sales for the band, this kind of thing."

Jim says his mother had three lives: Her childhood as a semi-slave for her family was the first. Her second was wife and mother. "She was certainly the nurturer. There was discipline in my life but I can say candidly that I would probably be better off if there had been more. My father was a travelling salesman and he spent every Tuesday and Thursday night out of town. He administered discipline on occasion."

But it was Dorothy who bore most of the responsibility of raising him in a small town in the northern Ozarks. "She was always there. When I went to junior high school she would drive me to school and pick me up. There were always well-cooked meals. If I needed help she was there. One time I played the part of George Washington in a school play and she made the costume for me including a three-cornered hat."

Dorothy's third life was as a widow living alone. That life lasted 34 years.

Jim went off to college and the Army and came home to begin a life in radio. He describes himself as a bit of a ladies' man in those years. "I'm not quite sure how that happened. It coincided when I began to drink to excess."

Then he met Camille, his first wife. "She was a diplomat's daughter. She worked in radio in Washington and she worked as a security guard at Sears, which helped her avoid a poverty-level existence." He was 26 when they were married.

What did Camille do for him? "There was a certain element of stability that accrued." She smoothed his rough edges. He learned to live with another person. "It involved the usual compromises and learning to give and take. Neither one of us was particularly demanding." The marriage lasted sixteen years. "We grew apart," he says.

How did that happen? "I don't know. Maybe immaturity."

In 1995, Jim, now a popular radio talk show host, was invited to station KFRU in Columbia, Missouri, to help celebrate the station's 70th anniversary on the air. One of his childhood schoolmates was working in Columbia. Her roommate wanted to meet Jim. The childhood schoolmate replied, "I've met him. It's no big deal." The friend insisted. "Get in the car, we're going," Jim relates. "It was a cold, icy, nasty night."

The childhood friend was named Annabelle. "We were students in bands at our elementary schools. She played flute.

I played trombone. We graduated from high school in 1962. Thirty- three years with no communication. Not a Christmas card. Not a phone call. Nothing."

They met at the radio station event and talked. They met again. "We started dating." They've been married for 18 years. What has she brought into his life? "A great deal of stability, I would say. A lot of detail. She's concerned about the house, that sort of thing."

Of course, there's more than that to a marriage that is lasting into their retirement. "It's a natural process of working together and living together. You become more like, in that regard, a business partnership. Finishing sentences and that sort of thing."

They live on a lake in South Carolina and breath the air of those who know they no longer have anything to prove. Life is more relaxed, even though Jim still does a three-hour nationwide talk show every night.

So, after all this time, what has he learned about women? "How little I know. How much I don't know."

Twenty-one

People are different based on their background and experience.
Lamont Gibson

Lamont Gibson has grown philosophical about women. It's the residue of two bad marriages. But he's split on his feelings about the women in his life. Wives, not so positive. Mother and grandmother, very positive.

"I would have to say my mother was the most important woman in my life." Six of the seven men in this book have said that. Lamont's mother, as we learned in an earlier chapter, became pregnant with him when she was in college. She was forced to drop out because that is what young women did in those days when they found themselves in that condition. She went to Chicago where she had relatives and there Lamont was born. Four years later she took him to live in Cleveland, where he grew up.

"She was dedicated to work. To achievement, accomplishments. She was serious about education. She had friends who were very well educated at the time. Women friends. So I was exposed to people who had college degrees."

She instilled in him a respect for education and work. "She was a no nonsense person. It was her way or the wrong way. I respected her highly."

She was hard on him. Lamont says she was not hard on his younger brother. "She was easy on him and that turned out not to be good for him. She was tough on me which turned out to be very good for me." Why was she easy on the brother and hard on Lamont? "I don't know. People have different types of love for different kids for different reasons."

He spent the first four years of his life with his grandfather in Montgomery, Alabama. His biological grandmother had died and his grandfather had married again. "The woman he married was an extremely warm, kind and loving woman. She introduced loved and affection into my life that you rarely see. When I went back to Montgomery she was always there."

These were the women who nurtured him, who protected and guided him to become a successful, educated man. But it would be a rocky journey once he left home. His life with women his own age began in high school in Cleveland. He had a sweetheart. He graduated and went into the Air Force. She pressured him into marrying her before he shipped out. It was a mistake.

"I think there was some expectation that I might not make it back and she might get something, so now was the time to get in line to get it." He survived Vietnam and came home to a marriage that didn't work. "We were a couple that couldn't live together or stay together. It did not work at all." Before the marriage ended they had a child, a son. He died as a young man. Lamont will not discuss it.

A year after the divorce he met wife number two at a party for teachers in Prince Georges County, Maryland. That marriage lasted for twenty-three years. They, too, had a son, a very bright young man who was accomplished in school and in his work. He has mixed feelings about the woman. "Great mother, terrible wife," is how he puts it. "I really believe she was ill," he says. The details are not as important as his conflict over the experience. "She helped me when I needed help." But then he will lapse into a story that shows his attitude is mostly negative. Soon he will come around to the pride he has in the son they had together.

He never married again. He's had relationships and was in one when we talked. "My relationships typically last a long period of time. I date women who are positive and good."

Now, after the early nurturing and the later unhappiness, what has he learned about women?

"My first wife was black. My second wife was Italian. I have dated Hispanic women, women from the Islands. I have had women of different nationalities. It's about the person. It's not about race. It's about attitude and how they treat you."

Race, he says, plays a part in attitude. "When I grew up white women were given a better life than black women. Black women grew up in an environment of injustice, racism. Many black women grew up in an environment where black men were incarcerated for many reasons. That impacted how they looked at life."

White women of that era typically grew up in homes where there was a dad who had a job and supported the family. Many black children grew up in homes where dad was in jail and couldn't find a decent job when he got out. In that respect, not much has changed in the intervening decades.

"People are different based on their background and experience," he says. He challenges my question about what he's learned about women. "I don't have a broad sweeping attitude about women. I don't think it's right to say I understand women. I understand people."

Twenty-two

I was 21. She was 18.
Johnny Holliday

I began this section of the book with a love story and I will end it with another one. Johnny and Mary Clare Holliday have been married for fifty-eight years as of this writing. But before I get to the love story there are two other women in Johnny's life who were important in his life: his mother and his grandmother.

Johnny's mother was named Dorothy Holliday. She was a dancer in her youth, a "knockout" as Johnny describes her. She and her sister performed dance routines in the Miami area. Her sister went to Hollywood and appeared in movies. "My mother decided to stay home and get married."

The early years of his life were good. "She was a wonderful homemaker and a terrific cook. She could make those Sunday dinners with fried chicken and mashed potatoes with candied yams. She made my favorite dessert, banana pudding with vanilla wafers in there."

Dorothy "was tough but she wasn't that tough. She always encouraged me. I was not a very good student. I got by. I was just interested in playing sports and singing in the choir and doing everything but schoolwork. I would get bad report cards and she would say keep trying. She kind of kept me on track and helped me get through school."

Then were was Gramma Bobbitt. "We would have dinner with her once a week. She was always so sweet. She was always the grandmother type. Soft spoken."

Life was sweet in those early years. Until, as Johnny says, "they both (his parents) got sick from drinking and carrying on." His father lost his job with Phillip Morris and took a job driving a beer truck. His health was bad and Johnny had to take off from school one day a week to help him on his routes. His father lost that job and the one after that. Then the family lost their home and had to move in with Gramma Bobbitt and her husband. Johnny was a senior in high school. "I was so embarrassed by that." Today, looking back, he says, "It was a terrible childhood."

The drinking and the cigarettes took their toll. Both of his parents died of cancer, his father at fifty-seven and his mother at sixty-nine.

Johnny graduated from high school and got a job delivering parts for a car dealer. One of the benefits of the job was a shirt with his name on it. He made $41 a week and life was good again. It got even better.

A friend was dating a girl who had a friend named Edgar Smith. "He says, hey, let's go to the beach. I want you to meet this girl. We go to the beach and these girls are sitting on a blanket. One of them was reading a magazine. Edgar, my friend, says, 'I want you to meet my friend here Johnny Bobbitt.' She put down her magazine and said 'hello' and went back to the magazine. I thought I have to follow up on this." He had just met the love of his life. Her name was Mary Clare. She was still in high school.

They dated for a year or so before he went up to Perry, Georgia, to work at his first radio job. He told her she could see other guys but she said she had no desire to do that so she waited for him to come back to Miami. He did, during her senior year. They decided to get married when she graduated.

"I had to ask her father. He was pretty stoic, very business-like all the time. We sat down. He was reading a paper. I said Mary Clare and I were thinking of getting married and wanted to ask his permission. He said, 'What do you do?' I said I'm a disc jockey. He didn't even look at me, he just kept reading the paper. He asked how much money I made. I told him $75 a week. He said, 'It doesn't matter what I say, you're gonna do it anyway.' We told him, no, not if you object. He said, 'Yeah, go ahead.' That was pretty much it."

They were married two weeks after Mary Clare graduated from high school in 1958. They moved to Rochester, New York, farther north than either of them had ever been. They had almost no furniture, little money, and no experience as married people. "We didn't have anybody around to go to. We couldn't go see Mom and Dad. We didn't have that." They grew up together. "Everything was trial and error."

They moved from city to city as Johnny's career developed. They had three daughters. They have grandchildren. And they are still together after all these years.

"It's been a lot of luck. A lot of laughing at each other and ourselves. It's pretty interesting that we've been able to do this. We've been so fortunate to have done all the things that have been right. There's no magic to it. You try to do the best you can. We've always had a good time."

What has Mary Clare meant to him?

"I wouldn't be where I am today without her, without her going along with everything I've done. The moving. Rochester. Cleveland. New York. San Francisco. Washington. Bringing up the girls because I was gone so much, working to get to that next level. I was not around as much as the average father would be. Anything the girls have done today is because of Mary Clare. She's a great mom. She's gone through more traumas with me than most wives do with their husbands. She's so understanding. She gets along with everybody."

Every man in these stories has had his life shaped by women, good or bad. Not one of them has given up his love of females.

Seven

The Men Who Taught Them How to be a Man

The superior man is distressed by the limitations of his ability; he is not distressed by the fact that men do not recognize the ability that he has.
Confucius

Twenty-three

I learned that I was a pretty good person.
Johnny Holliday

It is hard to overstate the importance of men in the lives of boys. Our mothers nurture us, feed us, help us with homework and make sure we take baths, but it is the men boys watch and learn from as they mature into men themselves. They are the examples by which boys learn how to be men. It would be nice - perfect even - if dads were the primary role models in this learning. That is not always the case. Take a look at American society today and the staggering number of single mothers and ponder the future of the boys they are raising. If these boys do not have positive male role models they may very well find negative models to imitate.

The good news is there are positive role models for boys whose fathers have failed to be there. Some of the men in this book are examples of how a boy deprived of a father's guidance can become successful not only in his career, but in his parenting.

We will begin with Johnny Holliday, whose love story with Mary Clare is still going on. Johnny grew up in an alcoholic household in Miami. His father lost one job after another. They lost their home and had to move in with his grandmother.

"She lived out of the North Miami school district so I had to hitchhike to school every day. A choral teacher named R. Watson Dutton picked me up at the same spot every day and took me to school. If I came right home after school he would take me home because he went right by my house. If not, I would hitchhike."

Mr. Dutton gave Johnny more than a ride. "He taught me how to sing. He had me do solos in the choir." He told Johnny not to be nervous and that he had the entire choir to back him up if he forgot the words. The lesson Johnny learned here was that the teacher had faith in him.

Then there was his baseball coach, Jack Clark. Mr. Clark showed that he had faith in Johnny by giving him the ball as the starting pitcher in the first game of the first season of baseball at North Miami High School. Johnny was not the best pitcher. In fact, he was very wild with his pitches and he would only last one inning. But the coach told Johnny that he was effective because opposing batters had no idea where the ball was going. Another lesson learned. Another positive message.

His basketball coach instilled a sense of pride and teamwork. "He would tell us, 'If you look at this basketball team, you're one of eleven guys representing this school. That's how good you are. You are all very good. And you are good people and you're only going to get better.' When you're not the star of the team you think about that a lot. I'm a small guy but he would make us feel like we were as important as anybody else on the team. He probably instilled in me the most confidence."

The coach's name was Fred Hyrne. "He was a religious guy and he taught Sunday school and got me to go to his church. I didn't have any affiliation at all until I married Mary Clare. I'd rather be out playing ball or go to the beach with my buddies than go to church. He got me to go to church."

After high school Johnny got into radio and credits his first bosses at a Miami station with giving him confidence to move up. "Harry Trenner and Herb Schore owned the station. Arnie Schore was Herb's son. Arnie, he's the one who talked to me about a job. He's the program director. He's only two years older than me. He said, 'I knew at your young age that you had something. The sky was the limit.'"

All of this was oxygen to Johnny and it gave meaning to his life. He got lessons in how to be a man from guys who were not family members. "My father started going downhill when I was in the eighth or ninth grade. You kind of turn your head because you see how other families are. When you get that sauce in you everything changes. They become angry. They become defensive."

His dad came to some of the games but Johnny lived in fear that his father would show up drunk. He never did. Sometimes he was too drunk to go to the game. Other dads came and Johnny wondered what it would be like to have a dad who was like those men. Today Johnny recalls that it was his father who taught him how to pitch. Despite everything, his voice softens when he talks about his dad.

Johnny has had a long and loving marriage, three beautiful daughters, grandchildren, and a happy family life. The men who cared about him when he was boy lived long enough to see him succeed. They saw him grow into a man to be proud of, even though his own father failed him. "You do it with other people," says Johnny.

Twenty-four

"Don't give up. Hang in there.
Do what it takes to succeed."
Jim Bohannon's dad

Small acts can have a life-long impact on someone you've never met. Jim Bohannon's life, his career, was shaped by men he knew and one man he never met. But Jim also worked hard and recognized an open door when he saw one.

The earliest male influence on his life was his father, Everett. Jim describes him as "a hard-working man, a simple man, not totally unlettered. He was a travelling salesman, not deeply involved in the issues of the day, but he certainly set a standard of hard work, persistence and honesty." His dad was in a near fatal car accident in the 1952 and was laid up for months. His boss continued his paychecks even though Everett was unable to work. It was a generous act that Everett never forgot.

"He never made more than $6,000 a year in his life. He never got a day off and he never got a vacation," Jim says. His boss's name was Bud Clark. He owned a small business and Everett was one of his salesman. He was so loyal to Bud Clark that he turned down an offer to make $25,000 a year at a business in Springfield, a small city about fifty miles from Lebanon. It was good money for the time and would have bumped the Bohannons to nearly the upper middle class. Jim says he appreciates his father's loyalty but he adds, "He showed a lot more loyalty to Bud Clark than he did for my mother and me." Jim concedes that as a boy he never wanted for anything but he says, "I never wanted very much."

Another male influence was Jim Abbott, a speech teacher at Lebanon High School. Jim had no real interest in speech class until another girl talked him into it. "I took that course. That led to the Lebanon High School debate tournament where you had to host various events. Of course, the seniors got all the good events like debate and extemporaneous speaking. I was left with two choices, radio and poetry reading. I couldn't take poetry reading because that would have set back my puberty. So I was left with radio speaking, which sent me to KLWT to collect wire copy. I put my nose to the glass and looked in. That was the beginning of my radio career."

KLWT's call letters, at least among its audience, stood for Keep Listening, We're Trying. The station was run by a man named Jack Sellers. He hired Jim as a part-time announcer, which, as we learned earlier, greatly improved Jim's social life in high school. When Jim graduated, Jack wrote Jim a letter of recommendation. It was not the most glowing endorsement:

"This is to inform you that Mr. Jim Bohannon has worked with us on a part-time basis for the past two years. We have found his work to be satisfactory and he shows an interest in broadcasting. His voice is pleasing on the air and he does a good job in conducting a program."

Today a job rating of "satisfactory" would not be seen by prospective employers as high praise, but it was enough to get Jim his next job. He had taken the first steps in a long and successful career.

Here is where we get to the part that Jim could never have planned. By 1981 Jim was hosting a talk show on WCFL in Chicago. Larry King, whose nationwide radio show had begun three years earlier, came to Chicago to do his show for one night, using a WCFL engineer. The engineer spent the night telling King how great this guy Bohannon was. That was in the spring of '81. King had scheduled a night off for the fall of that year and his regular backup, Jim Slade, was to fill in. Slade was also the space correspondent for Mutual Broadcasting, the network that employed King. NASA had a rocket launch scheduled for the same time. Slade would cover the launch from Cape Canaveral and hustle back to Washington to fill in for King that night.

Fate stepped in. "This mechanic left a wrench in the rocket and the launch was delayed. Mutual wanted to keep the coverage going. Slade couldn't fill in, so somebody said what about this guy Bohannon. Larry had said good things about me. That's how I was picked to fill in for Larry for the first time and that led to a full time gig at Mutual. That was a big impact on my life." Larry King left the radio show in 1994 and Bohannon took over. It has given him a nightly audience in the millions.

His dad, the speech teacher, the radio station manager, a radio engineer, Larry King, and an unknown mechanic at Cape Canaveral. Each held, in his own way, a sign pointing Jim Bohannon to his next stop.

And there's one more. "A guy I knew in the Army. Very intellectual. A world champion drinker. One day he stopped drinking. I suppose it was he who convinced me I was drinking too much. That was a major impact on my life."

Twenty-five

You do the right thing because it's the right thing to do.
Jim King's dad

Some of the men in this book didn't mention their dads until they were prodded and only then did they find some lesson they had learned from the men whose genes they carry. Not so Jim King. His dad was the first and only man he thought of when I asked him who were the most important men in his life.

"Hmmm. You know, only my father. I can't think of any teachers, male teachers, or anything like that. My father was the dominant figure in my life. I was an only child. I ended up hearing my father come out of my mouth when I was yelling at my kids."

Quessell King, named after a famous Frenchman, grew up on a Virginia farm. "He grew up tough, physically tough. He left school in the ninth or tenth grade. The family was always poor. Lots of kids. Never had enough money to file an income tax return."

He left the farm to join the Civilian Conservation Corps, a depression era program.. The CCC was the most popular of the New Deal programs of the Roosevelt administration during the 1930s. It put young men to work building parks, roads, bridges and other projects in America's wilderness areas, cities, and everywhere in between. It paid the men $30 a month and required them to send $25 of those dollars home to their families. In the nine years of the CCC's existence three million men constructed more than 800 parks across the country and improved state parks. They fought forest fires. They built a network of roads in remote areas, including the famous Skyline Drive in Virginia.

"He ended up in D.C. building Fort Dupont Park in Anacostia. It was quasi military. Hard physical labor."

The war came and he was drafted. He fought in Europe, came home, used the GI bill to go to school to become an electrician, and settled into a blue-collar life.

"He was hard-headed in a lot of respects," Jim says, but he taught his son about life, at least as he saw it. "He had definite ideas about right and wrong. Do your work. If it's worth doing, it's worth doing right. Standard American 'let's get the job done.'"

And what did Jim learn from Quessell King? "Consistency. Common sense. Do it right. No big philosophical thing. Kind of the working class way of life. You do the right thing because it's the right thing to do."

It's a theme in his life. Asked what lessons about being a man he learned from his father, he was quick with an answer. "To be a man is to do the right thing. Even if it's hard, you do it. You may not get anything out of it financially but you have your personal pride and the knowledge that you did the right thing."

These are the bedrock values that Quessell passed to Jim who passed them to his son. "Take care of your own. Take care of your family. Pay your taxes. Obey the law."

These values may not play well in today's world where gaming the system is an assumed attribute of the sophisticated crowd. Values about hard work and honesty may be seen as old fashioned by people who have become cynical about present day America. But there are those like Jim King who still live by these values and he believes his son does as well.

"You read something in the paper, somebody stole money, and you think, you idiot, you stole money, you deserve to go to jail."

He adds that he's not cruel in his judgements. "If somebody makes an honest decision and they're wrong, I can understand that. We all judge based on situations. Why did the guy steal bread? His family was starving. I can understand that. It depends on the situation but I judge people on those values."

There will be more about values later.

Twenty-six

***I keep negative men, negative women out of my life.
Lamont Gibson***

Lamont Gibson is a successful man by any standard. Despite racism and exposure to gangs as a boy in Cleveland, he has managed to use his intelligence and drive to rise above the negativity around him and find the positive models that propelled him upward.

He spent his summers with his grandfather in Montgomery, Alabama during a time in which black Americans had few rights in the Deep South. His grandfather was a man to be reckoned with and gave Lamont strong lessons in how to succeed in life.

"He was a positive influential figure. He owned six houses. He was smart financially. He was the kind of adult that any person would look up to. He retired from the railroad and had a comfortable business in real estate. He treated people well. I didn't gather a lot of negative things from him."

It was something that would be a hallmark of his life. "I was fortunate enough to be around some very successful black men. They were role models."

He was also around white men who were eager to help a smart young man, no matter his color. "I was twenty-seven. I worked for a three-star general at Quantico Marine base. These men at that time, they were all white men. They talked to me. They would make recommendations and suggestions."

He was at Quantico during a critical time for the military. "I was there when the Marines promoted the first black to be a one-star general. I knew him. He became a very distinguished gentleman after they sent him to what they called charm school. I had another close friend, a drinking partner of mine, who became a U.S. ambassador to an African country. He was one way when we sat around talking and another way when he was in a business setting. He spoke what we call the Queen's English. He spoke clearly and distinctly. Listening to the people around me made a difference in the way I acted and the way I carried myself. I was fortunate to be put in situations where there were positive men. They would talk to me."

Lamont was a young man who paid attention to the men around him. "Even when I was young the old guys would say either you're going die or you're going to retire. Plan for retirement." He did. He now lives in comfortable retirement. "My favorite joke is when I was younger I had a six- pack and now I have six-figures."

Lamont, like most men of the older generation, grew up hearing versions of the phrase "Be a man" or "Act like a man." What does that mean to him?

"In different settings it means different things. I listen to who's saying it. If it's a sister from the hood who's saying it, she wants somebody to take care of the work around the house, the man's work. And she may want somebody to pick up a bill or two and that's the man's job, to take care of his woman. If it's a very successful black woman, and I've been fortunate enough to know a number of those, they mean a positive attitude, someone who knows how to act like a distinguished gentleman and not embarrass them in public. A man who can speak on most subjects knowledgeably."

Lamont doesn't see a man's role as dominant or domineering. "I never saw it as being the boss. I have always surrounded myself with strong women. I don't need to be the boss. They don't want to walk behind me. They want to walk beside me. I never let anybody walk in front of me."

He's seen plenty of bad role models, men whom he did not want to emulate. "I knew men who went to jail, to prison. I knew I didn't want to be involved in drugs. I didn't want to be involved in crime that would send me to jail. I knew that I was not going to beat on a woman. The men that I knew that beat their women I totally disliked."

You may have noticed that Lamont did not mention his father or stepfather. It's not something he wants to discuss.

Twenty-seven

It's like ranking paintings in a top flight museum.
Grady Smith

Grady Smith, the Army officer and arts scholar, credits a long list of men with helping him become the man he is today. "That would shock all of the men. They would not consider themselves masterpieces," he says. Who are they? "Starting with my dad. Two priests in high school, my platoon sergeant when I got a platoon in the 82nd Airborne Division and later one of my full colonels."

First, his dad. "I did not realize how important he was for me as an influence on me in thinking, general behavior, and comportment for many years after he died." Grady had what he calls a crazy kid's dream of hunting and fishing. His father was not a hunter or a fisherman. "That was not his thing. He was a guy who did carpentry at home. He was very good at it. It took me years to realize that nobody can be all things to anybody." Grady says he learned a great lesson about his father during the darkest days of the civil rights movement. "I remember us sitting in front of the black and white TV watching the newscast on the riots in Selma, Alabama and Sheriff Bull Connor loosing dogs on an otherwise peaceful demonstration. My dad, who was born in rural North Carolina, looked at that and said, 'That's not right.' Boom." His father, despite his Southern upbringing, knew that Bull Connor was wrong in the way he treated the marchers in Selma.

And what he could not get from his father he got from others. "If I can't get what I need from the guy who happens to be my dad, I have to look around among the people of my acquaintance for the modeling I wanted. When I got married my father-in-law was one of the great hunters of Scott County Iowa." He had found his hunting and fishing buddy.

Grady learned important life lessons from two priests at the Catholic high school he attended. "Father Tom Albrecht was an English teacher and an advisor on the school paper. Father Larry Schieber was also a teacher and a guy to hang out with. Both of these guys were teaching me levels of communication that have held me in good stead all along. Father Tom was Steady Eddy, very methodical. Father Larry was more flamboyant, if you can say that about a priest. Father Larry, I remember him talking about a sermon he gave and one of the poems he quoted was "In Flanders Field." Larry taught sensibility and the need to look in a World War One poem for something that's relevant right now."

In Flanders Fields the poppies blow
Between the crosses row on row,
That mark our place; and in the sky
The larks, still bravely singing, fly
Scarce heard amid the guns below.

We are the Dead. Short days ago
We lived, felt dawn, saw sunset glow,
Loved and were loved, and now we lie
In Flanders fields.

Take up our quarrel with the foe:
To you from failing hands we throw
The torch; be yours to hold it high.
If ye break faith with us who die
We shall not sleep, though poppies grow
In Flanders fields.

"In Flanders Field" is one of the greatest war poems ever written. Its author was a Canadian surgeon named Lieutenant Colonel John McCrae. The poem was written following one of the most horrible battles in a terrible war that produced the slaughter of an entire generation of young men on all sides. It is fitting that the poem had a lasting impact on a young man whose career would be devoted to soldiering.

The next man on Grady's list is an Army sergeant in the famed 82nd Airborne Division. "Sergeant First Class Adams, we called him The G, for gorilla. When I reported to the company commander he called The G in and said, 'When you get him shaped up, give him back.' That's kind of what he did. He was not a pain in the butt. He led by example. He was so technically competent. He taught me things about leadership techniques and they're embedded in carriage and attitude. He said, 'Don't cop an attitude. We know you're an officer.' He took care of his men."

The final man on his list was a colonel, a bull colonel as O-6s are known. A second lieutenant is an O-1, the lowest officer rank. An O-6 is six positions up, a full colonel. A brigadier general of an O-7. "He would tell me stories. I began to absorb how to be polite and make tasks clear."

And so, after all these years, what does it mean to be a man? "Do the right thing comes to mind."

Twenty-eight

I can't think of anyone more influential than my father and my mother.
Jared Grantham

In many ways Jared Grantham's childhood was right out of Little House on the Prairie. Small town Kansas, fishing, listening to men tell tall tales. In the center of all of this was his father, Jimmy. "He was a good time guy. I could see the joy of life through his eyes. He really enjoyed being with people and looking after people."

Jimmy Grantham was a child of what was left of the frontier. He was born in Dodge City a few years after the town's wild cattle days but he had the energy of the West. He was a good dancer. He liked a nip now and then. As a young man he was not afraid of a fist fight, all in good-natured fun. He loved life.

"He was very generous. During the war he got ahold of some Hershey's chocolate bars. They were hard to come by. He gave them to a soldier he picked up in his truck. He could drive you nuts. On the other hand, you got the message of generosity."

Jimmy took Jared along on his truck route to western Kansas where he delivered propane tanks to towns that had no electricity or gas lines. "He was influential in my singing. He had a nice tenor voice. We sang songs all the time." And their time together was not limited to long drives across the high plains. "We would go fishing at night and he would talk about his hopes and dreams and we would sit there and swat mosquitoes. We never caught anything."

Jared's dad was someone everybody in town knew. "He was a Boy Scout leader, the first one in Johnson. He knew how to quiet boys down and get them to pay attention. He was a fellow everybody liked."

So what did Jared learn from him? "I learned how to dream and how to look at things from the other person's perspective."

Today Jared admits that maybe Jimmy was a little too easy on the boy. "I was spoiled. I tended to be a little too critical of my parents from time to time, which I now regret deeply. He didn't teach me that, it's just that he was so kind to me I took advantage of the situation."

Jared's polio brought another major influence into Jared's life. "My physician, Dr. Field. He made the diagnosis of polio. When I got out of the hospital he put me to work in his office and mentored me in terms of scientific interest. He was the greatest guy in the world as far as I was concerned. He was killed in an accident at the church. He was influential in terms of my being a doctor. He helped me develop my inquisitiveness. He taught me compassion. He was very thoughtful, honest, easy to talk to."

At Baker University Jared met William Rice, a voice coach. "He took me under his wing. He knew I had polio and had only one lung. He did everything he could to bolster my singing. He enrolled me in contests. I never won anything. And there was Dr. Alvin Boyd in the biology department. His love of science was infectious."

And so these men, his father, his doctor and his teachers, all set him on a path to become the man he is today. He concedes that the standards of manhood in Johnson, Kansas, way back then were not the same ones many men adhere to today.

"In Johnson, Kansas, nobody cared whether you could write a complete sentence. You could win a Nobel Prize and nobody would know that it was. Most people focused on athleticism or strength. They all had guns. I had guns as a boy. They were focused on hunter-gatherer types of ventures. They wanted to be protected and they wanted their guns nearby. They wanted to be personally strong. So strength, prowess, athleticism. That was legal tender for men. Once I had polio I couldn't possibly measure up to that. I was an oddball. I had to rely on my brain and vocal talents."

His brains have taken him to the highest levels of medicine. But he still acknowledges the basic value of a man's word is his bond.

Twenty-nine

Looking back at high school and college
I can't remember a single man that I trusted.
Tom Glenn

Tom Glenn all but raised himself. His father was a ne'er do well lawyer who stole from his clients, wrote bad checks, and died in a bar fight. His mother was an alcoholic and was unable to spend much time looking after him. Still, his dad, a man he grew to despise, taught him valuable lessons on how to be a man.

"All the things I shouldn't do. I shouldn't lie. I shouldn't fake. I certainly shouldn't embezzle $40,000. I should see to it that my clients respected me and I respected them. As I went on in life I saw to it that I respected other people and found that they respected me when I do that." Of all the men in this book only Tom cannot name one single man who was a positive influence on him when he was a boy. His experience growing up in a dysfunctional family did teach him lessons that he carried into his adult life.

"I promised myself that I would be a good father to my children. I would never do the things he did. In the ten years or so before his death I saw to it that he couldn't track me down because he had been writing bad checks against my checking account. I didn't want him to know where I was. I learned to be a good father. I took very good care of my children. I would never have deserted them the way he did me."

As we learned in earlier chapters, Tom put himself through college and earned a PhD. He had a successful career. He was a grown man before he found a positive male role model. "This guy was my boss at NSA during the Vietnam period. Don Jackson. He was the best manager that I had ever come across. He trusted his people. He was their support. He was down below lifting up his hands to help them achieve."

Finally, a man who offered a road forward. "The way he treated people. I thought that's the way to be a manager and when I became a manager I did the same thing. I did that all the way through to the very end when I was an executive. Always supporting the people, not trying to control them but trying to uplift them, trying to encourage them to be creative and do their very best. By God, it worked perfectly. I was not well liked at NSA because I was that kind of manager. I was well liked by my subordinates but not by the powers that be."

Maybe it was the generation that these men represent or maybe it was something else, but Tom, like the others, came of age in an era when the idea of "being a man" was passed to all young men. "I still have it with me today, this business of being strong and muscular and being able to do everything myself and not having to rely on other people. Since the onset of cancer it's been a real humiliation for me. I have to depend on other people and it's not what I'm supposed to do. I'm a man and I'm big and strong and I take care of other people. That's very much a part of my personality."

Today, in what is mostly an urban or suburban America separated by time from the rural frontier, the old idea of manliness is fading to a new model. "Young men today do not have nearly that much of a model engrained in them as I do. They're much better fathers. I see them in a supermarket, a father and a baby. I would never have done that as a young man. I took care of my children, don't get me wrong, but I wouldn't have dreamed of going out with my baby. That would have made me look feminine. They're much better off than we were."

He admits he was conflicted as a young father. He had the idea that a man didn't look after the children. That was the wife's job. "My wife had severe problems herself and she was not taking care of the children, so I had to do both. My feeling in those days was I had to support the family the best I could."

He has three daughters and a son. "I feel close to them but I don't see them very often." Although he feels he was a good father when his children were growing up, one daughter he doesn't see at all. "My second daughter has not spoken to me in thirty years. That was because the marriage broke up. The other three children all took my side and she sided with her mother and has not spoken to me since."

Part Eight

Parenting

We are made wise not by the recollection of our past, but by the responsibility for our future.
George Bernard Shaw

Thirty

Parenting is more than just putting food on the table and saying, "Oh what a nice job, Johnny."
Jim King

In the 1950s, when the men whose lives are being told in this book were kids, there were very few, if any, helicopter parents who hovered over every minute of their children's lives. We were told to go outside and play and don't come home until dinner. If we did something we weren't supposed to do another adult would tell our parents and we would face punishment. It's true that then, as now, some parents were terrible people and did terrible things to their boys and girls, but most of us lived with a range of parenting that was acceptable for the time, including a swat on the butt.

Jim King's dad was "hard," to use his word. He left home at seventeen to get away from him. But Jim grew into a man believing that parenting meant being a strong guide for his children. "Teacher, mentor, disciplinarian. Making sure children did the right things."

Jim and his wife took their parenting very seriously and he believes the guidance that children need begins very early. "Infants don't understand the concepts but they do understand no and yes and good and bad. You start that from the time they can respond to you. You start out getting a smile from a baby."

Parents, he says, need to be a constant in their children's lives. "Your children know that they can depend on you. Other things may change but mom and dad are always there and they will help you. They will yell at you. They will disapprove of bad and approve of good. They will value your judgement. It's an art. It's hard. It's like being a painter. Anybody can slap paint on canvas. To be a good painter you have to have the talent. The basics can be taught but not the finesse."

Today's fathers are praised for spending more time with their kids, taking them to the store, helping with homework, and generally being there. The fathers of today's fathers are often criticized for not being around, for spending too much time at their jobs and being cranky when they got home. Jim says there's something to that.

"I guess mom was around more than dad in those days. You work long days and when you came home you had to mow the lawn and fix the car, so mom was more involved in the child rearing. I was the strong arm. I was the threat. 'Wait until your dad gets home.' The boogeyman. That's a good thing for your children to learn, that there is some penalty for not doing right, maybe a slap on the butt or go-to-your-room. There are consequences. It didn't matter who was doing it, it was the fact that it was done at all."

This is where the generational split occurs between older parents and young ones. Maybe it's been that way since the dawn of time. The older people think the young people of today are too lenient. "That's the problem with the world. Some people have never really parented their kids. Parenting is doing the tough stuff of spanking or go-to-your-room. The punishment is as much of a pain to the parent as it is to the child. It's something that must be done and that's your job and it must be done right," Jim says.

Jim concedes that his own father thought he was too lenient with his kids but he says today his father, who lived into his nineties, was quite proud of Jim and his children. "He had nothing to be embarrassed about," Jim says.

Is he close to his children today? "I am. They live with me, more out of economic circumstances."

How did they turn out?

"Very well. I'm very happy. You always wish that they could do better but you always know they could have done worse. They made it to adulthood without doing something that could mess them up forever."

He's disturbed about a trend that today's young people have adopted. "I'm looking at these young people who are getting these tattoos and thinking that's something you can't get undone."

About his own father, he says, "He was been happy with me. I didn't go the way he wanted. He wanted me to become an electronics engineer. I tried but it didn't work out. At least I did something he was proud of." And as for his rocky relationship with his dad when he was a young man moving out of the house, he says, "We had a stormy relationship. Looking back it was as much my fault as it was his."

Thirty-one

I still feel guilty about whacking them on the butt.
Grady Smith

Spanking is no longer considered a proper parenting technique. In some circles whacking a kid on the butt is considered assault and there are those who think it should be subject to criminal charges. That was not the prevailing opinion when the men in this book were growing up nor was it considered evil when these men were themselves raising children. But times and opinions change and the men profiled on these pages feel bad about the whacks they inflicted on their kids.

Grady Smith is the first to admit he feels terrible about it. "My dad was the calm, quiet steady Eddy and mostly did not interfere with the child raising activities. That was my mom's job. She fed us, clothed us, spanked us and took care of us. I learned spanking from my mom. Between that and the attitude of discipline that I absorbed in the military, I'm not sure that was a good lesson to learn. Fortunately, I was off fighting wars for a couple of tours." This last comment was followed by a small laugh.

"I absorbed that approach and applied it. I was also a liberal user of go-to-your-room."

The generation that Grady represents carried on the parenting techniques that had been passed along for generations. The generation born in the early part of the twentieth century - Grady's parents and the others profiled here - had horror stories of their own childhoods and believed themselves to be much more moderate than their own parents. And even though Grady says he's sorry about the spankings he delivered, he's relieved that his own children did not carry on the family tradition. "I picked up my habits from my parents. My kids did not pick up my habits from me and that's probably good."

He admits that he focuses on the bad at the expense of the good. "My consciousness zooms in on the guilty stuff. I kind of forget or discount when I did something right, so I have to give myself the benefit of the doubt."

In the end, what is parenting all about?

"I think in the end stage analysis you've done well if your children are able to make good choices based on what's going on in front of them. That can be a small choice like what's for dinner or a big choice like who to vote for in November. It can be a huge choice like what do I want to do with my life."

Here is where Grady shows the pride he has in his children. "My son has an MFA in sculpture. That doesn't butter a lot of bread. But he is one happy camper. My daughter is happy. She was a dance major. She is now a human resource person focused on health benefits at her place. They chose their educational path. They chose their work path. They made good choices on their partners. My son's partner is an RN just finishing up to become a nurse practitioner. She was hoping to go into the Army to focus on PTSD. She did not meet the age requirement. This is the partner my son picked out. That's the choice he made. It's not that she was going to follow that path when he met her. It's that he picked a person who would do that kind of thing as a way of life."

His daughter from his first marriage lives in Atlanta and they have regular contact. "She's with a veteran of Gulf One, (the first Gulf war) who still has PTSD episodes. She helps him. These are my children and they all three have made really good life choices."

When he looks back to the days when his children were small and the family was living in Germany, he recalls the trips they made to the great sites of Europe. "I have a picture of my daughter at age three in the Louvre looking up at a huge painting. We took our kids to world-class museums. We took them to the Stuttgart Ballet." He recalls that his son, as a toddler, had a habit of falling into every fountain he touched. "Katy just threw a change of shorts in the car."

Still, in the end, he can't shake the feeling of regret over spanking them. He's thankful that he has a close relationship with them and that they are, in his opinion, much better parents than he was.

"I'm really proud of my kids."

Thirty-two

Whatever we had we put into our kids.
Johnny Holliday

It's a kind of cliché that one generation passes its bad parenting on to the next one. That simple thought is used to explain why generations are the way they are, good or bad. Upper class WASPs, we're told, pass along their class-consciousness to their children by sending them to the best schools. Lower class ne'er-do-wells do the same and hand to their kids a life of lazy slovenliness. The problem with this little bromide is it isn't true. Given the number of rags-to-riches stories in America and the overwhelming number of Americans who live better than their parents, it's misleading to think there's much to it.

Johnny Holliday is a perfect example. As we learned earlier, his childhood was terrible. His parents were not capable of giving him what he needed. He found a way forward on his own and he and his wife Mary Clare have raised three beautiful, successful daughters, all of whom were sent to the best schools and all of whom received everything their parents could offer.

Sometimes a difficult childhood where the examples are negative, not positive, provides incentives for how to do things right. I asked Johnny if his childhood carried over to his parenting.

"Oh, absolutely. We both (he and Mary Clare) have spent more time with our girls just trying to make sure we're doing the right things and trusting them. I told every one of them 'Don't let anybody tell you you can't do something because you're looking at a perfect example right here. I'm a person who had no shot at success. I had no college degree. I barely got out of high school. I had no idea what I wanted to do. But I hooked on to something and worked my tail off and I loved it and I made something of myself. With the education you guys have you're well ahead of the game. You can do anything.' Each of them has gone on to prove that."

Sending his girls to the best schools was not easy. Even though he was very successful in radio he never made big money. "I never started making good money until around 1980. I was in the lower echelon of disc jockeys and sports guys. There's the old adage 'You can do anything for your kids.' Whatever we had we put into our kids. That has given Mary Clare and I more satisfaction now that we see what they're doing with their kids."

He admits to the temptation that all grandparents experience, to interfere when he thinks his grandchildren need correcting. "There's that tendency to step in. Mary Clare will say 'This is not your child. Let their mom and dad discipline them if you think they're doing something wrong.'"

Many parents tell tales of their childhoods to their children. Some are of the "I had to walk five miles to school" variety. Johnny described the bad times to his girls to help them understand what they had. "Anytime I wanted to make a point, this was when they were young, and they would immediately start crying and say 'Oh my god, Dad.'"

It carried over into his discipline. "I would say the reason I'm concerned about you coming home late is because I would come home late and only bad things can happen if you're out late. I would tell them stories."

Sharing the same values is the key to his marriage and his parenting. He and Mary Clare have been together all of their adult lives. They agree on most things and worked together when the girls were young. "Oh, yes. She's tougher than I am. I would get angry sometimes at the girls and she would handle it in a much more (here he laughs) sophisticated manner."

Now, in his late seventies, Johnny has the satisfaction of a life well lived, despite his early years, and the pride that comes with successful children. "Oh my god. I am more proud of them than anything I've ever done. I'm proud of what kind of parents they are. I tell people you don't know that feeling until you have grandkids."

Johnny is as optimistic as anyone I've ever known. He stepped around and over obstacles that would have given others an excuse to sit down and let life pass him by. He chose not to. "The one thing I've always tried to do is put myself on the same level as whoever I'm dealing with. Consider the education I have, the background I have. Not much."

Thirty-three

I wish I could have been a better father.
Jared Grantham

Maybe a man's eighth decade is a time of regret or maybe it's just a better perspective, but the theme runs through many of the older men I know. It certainly plagues the men in this book. Parenting is a common regret, as Jared expressed in the quote above.

I will begin Jared's story back in far western Kansas. He was an only child until the age of fourteen when polio and his baby sister arrived in the same year. Both changed his life. Until then he had his parents all to himself and it was not always a happy home. What did he learn from them?

"Never argue in front of your children. They not only argued, they fought. They used horrible, abusive language to each other. It was really nasty. I would beg them not to do that. 'Don't! Please stop!'"

His father, Jimmy, was a good-time guy. His mother, Ista, was self-contained. They were oil and water. "My father was a very likeable guy. He loved dancing and kissing the girls. He would lean over to kiss my mother and she would lean away from him. They just had an extremely difficult relationship for many years. My father was frustrated with my mother and she was frustrated with him. They fed on their frustrations. I was caught in the middle."

Jared admits that his parents had a positive side, at least when it came to their son. "They would have both died for me. I was the focus of their existence. Had I not been there they would probably have been divorced. It wasn't until they were in their late fifties they had enough money to buy the cabin in Colorado." Jimmy and Ista drove through the mountains looking for a vacation spot in their brand new Chevrolet El Camino, a pickup truck disguised as a car. It turned into a romantic vacation. "He said, 'You know, she told me she loved me. That's the first time she's ever said that.'"

Jared believes that his parents fell in love only in the last ten years they were together, in the time before Jimmy died of cancer.

Jared's family is, from the outside, ideal. A successful dad, a wonderful mother, successful children with kids of their own. How would he grade himself as a parent?

"I would look at it in different stages. First stage I was in medical school, in residency. Janeane was born and then Taylor. As busy as I was I helped out as much as I could when I was at home. I was infatuated with those kids. I liked to be around them and I liked to hold them, except when they kept me awake at night. Carol had to get up with them because I had to get up and go to work the next day. Under the constraints of being a physician in training and a resident in medicine I would give myself a C or a C+."

For this medical school professor a C grade is the highest mark he will give himself as a parent. "It got worse as things went on, particularly my relationship with Carol. As the kids got older I expected her to do even more. I was going to the lab every day. I was beat. I came home and I gave them baths every night. Every Saturday morning I would take the older pair to the library for a couple of hours. I would give myself a C- or a D+ at that time."

His time at NIH over, Jared, Carol and the children moved back to Kansas City, where he joined the faculty at the University of Kansas Medical Center. It took up even more of his time. The children were older and the two oldest boys began "acting out," in his words. "They were driving Carol crazy and I wasn't there to help her. We didn't have a heck of a good relationship during that time. It went on for several years. I don't think I was a very nice person during that time."

He admits that one of the problem was his lack of sleep. "I only slept three or four hours a night for fifteen years. I probably slipped down into the category of D if not F during those years."

His oldest son was sent to live with Jared's parents in western Kansas, where he was removed from the environment that Jared blames on the young man's bad choices. "He found his way out of that environment he was in. Things got better between us." His second son went off to the University of Kansas, studied medicine, and now has a distinguished career as a cardiologist. He, too, made bad choices in high school but college turned him around. "He got into a fraternity that did not allow drugs, that kind of thing."

One event brought them all together and reminded them all of the value of family. Joel, the youngest son, was killed in a railroad accident. It was staggering loss that haunts the family to this day.

As he looks back at all that has taken place, Jared reflects on his role as a parent. "I think back a lot about it. I wish I could have been a better father. I really do. My intemperate behavior, I could have controlled better. I never hear about it from them. Carol and I do everything we can to support them."

Thirty-four

"I stayed in his life every day."
Lamont Gibson

Lamont is very proud of his son. Get him into a conversation and he may go fifteen minutes about the young man, how smart he is, how many scholarships he's had, the jobs he's been offered and so on. But Lamont is guarded. He had one son who passed away in his twenties and it's something he will not discuss. "It's something that's – when you lose a child, it's a great, great loss. There's no way to say what was going on."

He had another son, a product of a temporary relationship, whom he did not meet until the son was a grown man. This son had been in prison and needed help. Lamont provided that help, even buying the fellow a car, until he realized he was being played.

The son he talks about frequently is from his second marriage. "I talked to my son about success. I told him to respect everyone. I told him to read everything about the subject of a meeting before going to that meeting; to be prepared to ask intelligent questions at meetings; to demonstrate his intelligence and eliminate any discussion about his wealth of knowledge about the subject matter."

He talked to the boy about how to conduct himself in public. "I told to him about, you know, if you get stopped by the police and you're driving. Put both hands on the steering wheel. You don't fight the police because you think you're right. Some young black men think you can just talk back and say, 'You don't have the right to arrest me!' Those parents raised their kids to think they're the best thing since sliced pie and fight back and talk because they can't be done wrong. Sometimes when you fight back with the police you are causing a problem that otherwise wouldn't occur."

When you talked to your son did you tell him that as a young black man he's going to have people jumping out, blocking his way?

"Oh yes, oh yes. He told me, he said, 'I don't want to be a lawyer.' I said, 'You don't have to be a lawyer if you get a law degree. You get a law degree and doors are going to open for you. You get a law degree, you'll have improved yourself. And it makes it a lot easier for people to look to you and see certain things. You'll be highly respected.'"

Lamont's memories of his boyhood are still filled with images of an America that was cruel to minorities. "Today, policer officers will not be tolerated in doing things that they did as the norm when I was a kid. Police officers would rape young girls and no one would say anything. They would rob stores. Young boys, they could just beat them up or shoot them in the back. That kind of thing was common in Alabama."

By the time Lamont married his second wife he was well on his way to a successful career. He was also determined to be a good father. He does not have the regrets that other men in this book have expressed about not being around enough for his son.

"No, from the time my son was born, when he cried I was the first to jump up to go to the refrigerator and get the bottle and feed him. When he was in elementary school I would drive him to soccer practice. I was teaching him soccer. I was the one who was out there teaching him basketball, teaching him baseball. He was on a baseball team. I was making sure he got the team sport mentality. He understood what teamwork was all about. His mother focused on his studies. She was a scholar. She was well-educated."

Lamont's memories of his own boyhood influenced his behavior as a father, as it did for many men whose lives are being profiled on these pages. He wanted to be there for the boy and to help him understand the world. "I stayed in his life. Every day I had dinner with him. I was always there to talk to him, to be on top of him. I took him to kids shows at the Kennedy Center. I was in his life."

Thirty-five

I had the kids in Saigon with me, all four of them.
I got them out twenty days before Saigon fell.
Tom Glenn

It would be an understatement to say that Tom Glenn's children had an unusual childhood. Tom was a high level intelligence operative for the National Security Agency for over a decade during the war, spending time in and out of the country at a time when heavy fighting was taking place all around, and occasionally within, Saigon, the capital of what was then known as South Vietnam.

He and his then-wife first went to Vietnam in 1963 when they only had one child, a toddler. He met his wife at the NSA when they both were linguists. He was assigned back to NSA headquarters at Fort Meade, Maryland for a time but was then sent back to the war zone. By then they had more children.

"She was very anxious to go back and was not worried about the children. During the coup that killed the president she was caught at school, where she taught. The kids were at home with the servants looking after them. I made it home. I had to walk because I could not get a car during what was going on in the streets. She was not the least bit worried. The kids were in the middle of the room with the servants surrounding them to protect them from blasts that might occur."

His kids took life in a wartime capital as a normal part of life. All of their friends and the parents of their friends were in the same situation. "They didn't like Saigon. They didn't like the poverty, they were very aware of it. But they had a good life. Good schools. Plenty of people to play with, mostly French children at the beginning. Later there were more Americans. My oldest daughter grew up speaking French, Vietnamese and English."

Tom's children grew up in what anyone would describe as a rich childhood. That came to an end in April of 1975 as the North Vietnamese closed in on Saigon. He pleaded with his wife to take the children and leave. "My family flew out on the ninth of April." The city fell later that month.

"She wouldn't go unless I allowed her and the children to take a tour of the world. I said, yes, go." She took the children and headed west to Bangkok, Thailand, India, and the Middle East. "They had just gotten to Beirut when the (civil) war broke out. They managed to fly out before the airport was closed." The Lebanese civil war would claim a quarter-million lives and bring the beautiful city of Beirut to rubble. It would rage for fifteen years. Tom Glenn's wife and children fled the end of one long war only to find themselves at the beginning of another.

Tom barely made it out of Saigon with his life. He was sent back to NSA headquarters in Maryland where he and the children settled in to what would pass for a normal life. The marriage did not survive. One of his children sided with her mother and hasn't spoken to Tom in years. The other three sided with him. He is closest to his third daughter.

"She is quite open and critical of her mother. We had school plays and athletic events and she was never there, she was always going out to play tennis or to a coffee or tea or something. If anybody came it was me."

His kids lived the life of boys and girls whose parents are career intelligence operatives. "I remember coming home and they would say, 'What happened today?' and I would say I can't talk about it. When my kids were growing up the fact that I worked for the NSA was not public information. If someone asked what I did they would say, 'He works for the Department of Defense.'"

Tom's childhood was a nightmare of neglect and heartache. He vowed that he would be the best parent he could be and took his children with him even to Vietnam during the war. They had a privileged life in Saigon with servants, good schools, and status. The other things, like the war itself, were not as important as their day-to-day lives in an exotic city. The one thing they say about their father is that he did not spend his working life in a nine-to-five job selling insurance or huddled in a cubicle. He spent his working life saving the lives of his countrymen.

Thirty-six

I'm not that big on children.
Jim Bohannon

This chapter will be short. The man being discussed doesn't have any children and never wanted any. Choosing to fore-go parenthood is more common today than it was a few decades ago, when married couples were expected to re-produce and replicate their own families. Troll the Internet and most of the information about childless couples is about childless women, not men. We still regard childless-ness as a kind of affliction, although that's changing.

Jim Bohannon doesn't have kids. "It just sort of worked out that way. I guess you could call it by choice, yeah. There was never any deep discussion about it."

How do you feel about that now that you're in your seven-ties?

"Honestly, I'm not that big on children. I do, of course, have a stepdaughter and she's a lovely person, and a grown-up person too, but honestly when I'm around chil-dren, usually the thing I'm saying under my breath is, 'That was the smartest move I ever made.' I just don't find them enjoyable. I know some people seem to dote on every-body's kids, 'Oh, they're so cute!' Honestly, not to me. I do not for one moment miss the fact that I don't have any, not one moment."

Estimates about men who don't have children are all over the board. It seems to be around ten per cent, lower than the percentage of childless women. Men, after all, have a fundamental and primal desire to spread their seeds. Okay, maybe not to the extent that they produce offspring they must raise and support.

It's refreshing to listen to Jim express a feeling that many fathers have at one time or another felt but didn't express as well. "Children are an amazing hassle. They take up your time, they destroy the rhythm of your life, they cost a ton of money. You've got to really, really want something that comes with those side effects. I don't. I don't hate kids but to me they've always been a negative, negative, negative. I would have done my best to not show that to the kid or take it out on the kid, but it would have been a tough job on my part. I don't know why people want them, I really don't. I know that some do, and thank God we produce enough to perpetuate the species. But no thank you."

The reality is that not everyone is cut out to be a parent and some of those who are not raise children anyway and do it badly. Read the stories of the men in this book and you will find examples of bad fathers and mothers. Jim acknowledges that he would not have been a good dad and he is honest enough to not only say it but understand that by passing on the parenting thing he has done not only himself but a child a big favor. There's a lot to be said for that.

Part Nine

Values and Ethics

A man without ethics is a wild beast
loosed upon this world.
Albert Camus

Thirty-seven

Some people bring happiness and joy* wherever *they go.
Other people bring happiness and joy* whenever *they go.
Lamont Gibson

What are values, anyway? The National Defense University, which trains high level military leaders, says values and ethics are extremely broad terms. The leaders who are tasked with protecting the nation from external threats are advised that values include *"integrity, professionalism, caring, teamwork, and stewardship."* They are further advised that *"values determine what is right and what is wrong, and doing what is right or wrong is what we mean by ethics. To behave ethically is to behave in a manner consistent with what is right or moral."*

That is a good starting point. Obviously, military leaders face decisions most of us would never come across but the lessons are the same. These values and ethics are products of generations of experience and mistakes and, occasionally, triumph.

It's easy for older people to look at the new crop of young people and mutter something about how the younger generation doesn't measure up, that they don't have the values of decades ago and the world is going to hell.

Let's begin with Lamont Gibson.

Are today's values worse than they were when you were young?

"Values today are different. I don't think they were better then. I think that older men, older women, grew up during an era when punishment was everywhere. If you did wrong you could go to school and get the 'board of education.' They would paddle you. The teachers could paddle you. Or in the community your mother's neighbors could complain and grab a switch and hit you with it. People didn't hesitate to try and correct a kid. Today parents are over-protective of their kids. The kids grow up thinking they're God's gift and no one can touch them and they disrespect authority." Okay, maybe there is a hint of the old guy mumbling about how today's kids are brats.

His own childhood was not without its punishments for doing wrong. But he says that helped shape his values as an adult. "It's about how you grow up. It's about the community you grow up in and the parenting you receive."

How does that shape values? "It's how you define values and how you define what's right and wrong. If you were raised in an environment where you have to take, take, take and fight, fight, fight your values are different from someone who grew up in a loving environment."

As we saw from the National Defense University's definition of values, they define what's right and wrong. In earlier chapters the men used the phrase "do what's right." How is that defined?

"I think that trying to treat people well, treat people around you well. That's doing the right thing. (Doing wrong) doesn't have to be an attack that's against the Ten Commandments. It can be an act that hurts people. Abusing people verbally, that's basically wrong. You don't have to be a religious person to treat people right," Lamont says.

During the 2016 election cycle the news was filled with reports that Americans are angry and are looking for ways to express their anger. Lamont agrees. "I think there's a lot of anger in our society today, hatred and anger that people hid when I was younger. People are allowed to scream out their anger and their hatred. I just feel the wrong thing to do is preach hatred and anger. The right thing to do is preach happiness and love and make the people around you happy."

He referred to the anger and hatred that was once kept hidden from public view in communities that suffered from unfair and unequal social policies. He grew up in one of those communities, the black neighborhoods of Cleveland. But he says a bad experience in the past is no reason to spend your life in hatred.

"A large part of it is personal attitude. It's not only the way you grew up it is the attitude you adopted as an adult. Some people make themselves who they are. As an adult they decide who they are going to be."

What about respect?

"I have mixed emotions about respect. I do. I think that respect is necessary in a job environment because it's a part of what people think of you. However, there are certain things that people can do that don't merit much respect. You can't say 'I forgive you, it's all right if they harm you.'"

Treat people right. Do the right thing. Stand up for yourself. Lamont's values.

Thirty-eight

When everything is gray, everything is negotiable, nothing is truly of top value.
Jim Bohannon

Jim Bohannon is not a religious person. He does, however, concede that the values he lives by were formed when he was a young boy going to church in Lebanon, Missouri. Lebanon is a small town in the northern Ozarks and during the 1950s reflected the values of middle America. Hard work, honesty, keep your word, go to church. There were not many gray areas when it came to personal behavior. There was no such thing as situational morality, which allows us to make our own rules regarding moral issues. Indeed, situational morality disparages the word "morality" as judgmental and hurtful to people who have their own ideas of how live, however selfishly it might appear to others.

"It was a separate time. People did cling to certain immutable values. They hadn't been taught that everything was relative and the like. It was easier to make it through life if you knew with certainty that this was right and that was wrong. That's the short answer. I will grant you that life does have a lot of gray areas and it was an attitude that probably ignored some reality."

Those who believed in absolute right and wrong could be blind to the suffering of those who disagreed or were outside the mainstream. It was not until the sixties that large numbers of Americans began to challenge the status quo and demand more rights for minorities and women. Those who believed in the absolute rightness of the status quo pushed back and the social tension of that decade still resonates today. It appears that the champions of change won the war, if not all the battles. So now we have many areas of contemporary life that are "situational" in their values and the tension is being played out in areas where transgender issues, marriage and personal freedom are battle grounds.

It can make it appear as though there are no values at all. "Today's attitude that everything is gray ignores another reality and that is when everything is gray and everything is negotiable and nothing is truly of top value and that's not good, either."

So what does Jim value most?

"I suppose the first would be honor. I would like to be known as someone you can trust, someone who is honest."

And second?

"Second is a certain amount of security. I would like to know that when I got off to work I will come back alive and be reasonably well-compensated. I am not a great risk taker or one who has to get his adrenalin junkie fix like skydiving. Honor, to be trusted, and security. Those are pretty much the basics."

As a person who does not believe in God, how did he come by these values? "I came by them early on. It was later on that I adopted a more humanist viewpoint. I don't really need a cosmic boogyman to keep me in line, although clearly a lot of people benefit from that. In the beginning, I did and I wasn't disabused of such thoughts until I was a teenager."

What roles do values play in Jim's everything life?

"I hope they keep me on a straight and narrow and productive path. Obviously there have been many, many occasions when I've fallen short in all that, but at least they are there to return to and act as a standard along the lines of one's reach should exceed one's grasp. They are your compass, your chart. I know where I'm going and I know how I would like to get there."

Thirty-nine

I'm a knee jerk liberal
Grady Smith

Values are often shaped by time and experience. When Grady Smith was growing up the world was organized into what's right and what's wrong. Black or white. There was very little tolerance for "do your own thing." Grady thinks he was born too soon. There was more personal freedom only a few years later and there was the defining event of his generation, the Vietnam War. It all comes together.

"There were many days when I was jealous of guys who were born only ten years after I was. That was a whole different approach to relationships and what to do with the war. Geez, Larry, what are your values when the country says we gotta go to war again and it's something like Vietnam, not as clear cut as something like 9/11?"

Vietnam hangs heavy over his life and his values. He recalls the Kent State shootings of May 4, 1970 when soldiers in the Ohio National Guard fired sixty-seven rounds at students protesting the Vietnam War. Four of the demonstrators were killed and nine others were wounded. It was a searing moment in a long period of domestic discontent with the war.

Grady was a combat veteran who had commanded infantrymen in the Mekong Delta but he grew to believe that the war was wrong. "One of my Nam buddies sent me an article from the Cleveland Plain Dealer and there's been a new analysis with modern technology of the tape recording of the Kent State shootings and they've pulled out a command, a voice command, to the Guard to get ready to fire. You're talking about values and I'm thinking how does this sync with this is an oppositional set of values. The war was pretty patently wrong, built on fake crises. And the pattern repeated again with weapons of mass destruction in order to get Saddam Hussein." That was the premise of the Iraq War, that Saddam had weapons of mass destruction and was prepared to use them. No such weapons were found. "It's the Tonkin Gulf lie all over again."

President Johnson used the so-called Tonkin Gulf incident to generate support in Congress to expand the Vietnam War. The lie was that the North Vietnamese Navy had attacked an American naval vessel. The truth was not clear at the time. Nevertheless, the deception received Congressional approval to greatly increase American presence in South Vietnam, which led to the deaths of tens of thousands of Americans, some of them under the command of Grady Smith. A man like Grady, with an artist's temperament, can reflect on such a thing for a long time.

He admits he is not the typical, conservative retired military officer. "I'm a knee-jerk liberal, you know, and that doesn't receive aid and comfort from the conservative element in the military establishment, but we tolerate each other very well and that, too, is a value, that mutual tolerance, whether you agree or not."

He is not only concerned about the morality of war. He is also aware of changes in society in general, particularly the rise in the number of single mothers who overwhelmingly live in poverty. "I've met several moms-to-be, pregnant knowing they're gonna bring a kid into the world and it's gonna be a cold day in hell, indeed, whan that child will have a modicum of a chance to participate in the American dream."

He believes that the problem is societal, evidence of a seismic shift in values in terms of sexual issues. There's no more "wait until you get married." "That's all gone out the window in our lifetime."

What does Grady think makes an honorable life?

"That's a come as you are question about everything you've ever learned in your whole life, clusters of your subconscious when you have to make a moral choice. That's true whether you're twenty-five or seventy-five." Clusters of everything you've ever learned. It is how Grady found himself in the Army, in Vietnam, in combat.

His ancestors fought on both sides in the Civil War. His father fought in World War One. An uncle in World War Two. A cousin was a Marine during the Korean War. Other male relatives served during peacetime. "I heard the call in '64 and I didn't think whether it was going to be a good war or not. I stopped teaching English and I put on a uniform."

Me: Are you comfortable with that?

"I am. The Army took as much as it gave. I'm glad I did it and I'm glad I didn't serve any longer."

Forty

The goodness of Christianity seeped into my bones
Jared Grantham

No profession places a higher value on ethics than medicine. Physicians are, by their choice and training, healers. Physicians by tradition take the Hippocratic Oath, a vow to abide by certain standards of conduct and professional behavior. Part of it reads:

I will apply, for the benefit of the sick, all measures which are required, avoiding those twin traps of overtreatment and therapeutic nihilism

The dictionary defines nihilism as "the rejection of all religious and moral principles, often in the belief that life is meaningless." Life, to a physician, is far from meaningless. It is the reason the doctor heals.

Jared Grantham's desire to heal began in Johnson, way out on the far western edge of Kansas. Moral relativism was not a philosophy anyone subscribed to. There was right and there was wrong. Black or white. Not much gray. For Jared, it was all contained in what he learned at church.

"The goodness of being a Methodist came out. I didn't understand all of that stuff when I heard the scriptures read. I remember being in the seventh grade. We got a Bible if we could memorize the Book of John. So I got a free Bible from some evangelical group that came by. Donnie Richard and I memorized all of the verses of John. We promptly forgot them."

What he did not forget is the message of love and compassion he heard and felt from the congregation. He admits that, even then, he was not particularly religious in the strict sense. “I have always had a strong undercurrent of going to church. I liked to sing in the choir and that’s why I went to church. I liked the fellowship of my friends. But I didn’t necessarily like all the falderal of the religion and the preaching and telling you you had to do this or you had to do that. The goodness of Christianity seeped into my bones along with the evidence of that in my father and my mother. My mother had her harsh side but she was deep down a very good person in terms of looking out for people. She took in her sister’s daughters and housed them and fed them for several years. It’s that kind of example, going along with the fact that I was going to the Methodist church that seeped into my soul and gave me an ethical and moral underpinning.”

As we learned in earlier chapters, Jared was strongly influenced by the beloved town doctor who took him under his wing when Jared was recovering from polio. He was also influenced by physicians who were not as compassionate. The University of Kansas medical school reinforced his desire to be a doctor who put patients first.

“I remember a professor telling me, ‘When you’re in a room with a patient, the patient is the most important person in the room.’ If somebody put their foot up on the bed he would yell at them to get their foot off the bed. ‘He’s paying for it, you’re not,’ he said. He insisted that you know everything about the patient. He was just ruthless in his patient-centered approach to medicine. I was taught as a physician, a student of medicine, these skills to make the patient feel like the most important person in the room.”

Jared laments that today’s young doctors are under too much pressure to be efficient to be patient-centered. “They are under pressure to see a new patient every fifteen or thirty minutes. They've also got to log everything into the computer, otherwise they're going to be sued or they won't get paid."

He carries his compassion over into his private life. He is generous to family and friends. He's generous to the Methodist church where he and his wife Carol attend services, even though he claims to not believe in God. He has not held that belief since his son Joel was killed.

He is spending his remaining days connecting with those he loves, which seems to include most people.

"I genuinely feel compassion for everyone."

Forty-one

I believe there are things that are absolutely correct and absolutely wrong
Jim King

We learned in earlier chapters that Jim King believes in the value of hard work and that anything worth doing is worth doing right. He served in the Navy, worked his way through college and spent his career as a police officer in Montgomery County, Maryland. He has what he describes as "blue collar values." How were those values shaped?

"By my parents, my family, the milieu I grew up in, blue collar, hard working ethics of the thirties and forties. I guess that's because of where my parents were coming from. They grew up in the Depression and World War Two. Hard times. Hard working. Frugal. I still go around turning out the lights. Save stuff. I might need that in the future. My parents were not from the throwaway society. You did what you could. You did the best job you could. You just kept getting up every morning and going to work because people depended on you; your wife, your children. You work hard, do your job right. When you get knocked down you get back up. That's where I got my values."

That is what got him through the loss of his little girl and, later, the loss of his wife. Get up every morning and go to work because people depend on you. There's no room for self-pity. There's no time to fall apart and hide under the bed. There's no tolerance of giving up. One foot in front of the other. Keep moving.

It fits into Jim's beliefs in the treatment of others. Everyone, he says, deserves respect until they prove they don't deserve it. "Being from a blue collar background, having been blue collar myself, I realized the guy who picks up the garbage deserves as much respect, if not more respect, than the wall street entrepreneur, because he's out there, he or she, going to work every day even though life is hard. He does it because he has to. I give as much respect to the laborer as I do to the executive."

In the previous chapter Jared Grantham said his personal ethics were shaped by the Methodist Church when he was a boy attending services with his parents. He is no longer a believer but those values are still with him. Jim King echoes that feeling, even though he, too, is a non-believer.

"Although I am not a religious person by any means, I believe there are things that are absolutely correct and absolutely wrong." He concedes there are gray areas but even in those circumstances right and wrong prevail. He uses an example from his days as a police officer.

"As say, a police officer, I can understand that someone is hungry and they steal bread to eat. I understand that and I am compassionate toward them. What they did was wrong and they have my sympathy. As a police officer I must still arrest them but I can be as kind as a I can in that process. But if someone steals just for greed, because they want a bigger television, that's totally wrong."

He has passed his values on to his children and is very proud of them. He lives by his values.

He, and the other non-believers in this book, do believe that the basic Judeo-Christian values that defined this country for generations are still valid, even if they do not agree with the "religious" elements that go along with them. Religion and spirituality will be explored in the next part of this book.

Forty-two

Helping others, loving others, doing good.
Tom Glenn

How do we come by our moral compass? For some, it's through a church or an adult who set a good example. But what if your parents are no help in deciding what is right and what is wrong? What if they set a bad example? What then? For Tom Glenn it was a personal journey to learn about values and ethics.

"I did them for myself. At age seventeen I decided I didn't want to have anything to do with my parents anymore. I figured I was on my own after that. I was going to shape my life in my own way, do whatever I wanted to and one of those things in my mind was the search for what was right or wrong."

Many young people are judgmental and believe in the absolutes that youth brings to developing minds. For Tom, judging others was not a priority.

"I was scared. I didn't have anything to fall back on. I was looking at other people and asking how I could be like them and be accepted by them. When I went to college at the University of California at Berkley there were lots of gay people around and right away I realized that I can't reject these people because they were just like me. The first time I discovered that a man and woman were living together I thought that's not right, we can't let that happen. But then I looked at them and I got to know them and I thought I can't judge that. How am I supposed to know what's right or wrong?"

He admits that there was some residual spillover from his childhood when he was a devout Catholic. His mother never went to Mass and his father drove him to church but didn't go inside. His dad reeked of liquor when he picked up Tom to drive him home. But some of the church's messages got into his mind. "I was raised a strict Catholic and that meant sex only occurred in marriage and only between a man and a woman and never outside marriage. As I grew older I found that that's fine in principal and only if things work out. But I don't know anybody whose life worked out so perfectly that they were freed from making decisions like that."

So at Berkley he learned tolerance. A decade later he learned a philosophy of life. "In my thirties I took management courses and discovered Douglas McGregor, a very humanist management guy, and I read Abraham Maslow, the humanist philosopher. That led me to the philosophy of Karl Popper. It was really Maslow who changed my life, along with Popper. (Popper) was a scientific philosopher but I loved his work. He started talking about how we have to distinguish between hard fact and understanding. That doesn't mean that understanding doesn't exist, which a lot of scientists say, that understanding isn't real. (They say) the only thing that's real is what's concrete and measurable. But Popper said no, the understanding side of the world is as important, probably more important, than the factual side. I loved that and was off and running with him. It's been reshaping and refining my own system of ethics since then about what I believe is right and wrong."

And how has that played out?

"I am getting more and more generous and, I supposed, more and more liberal as I get older. I am less willing to condemn anybody for the things that they do. The one rule is don't hurt anybody."

What are the things that Tom thinks are right?

"Helping others, loving others, doing good. Fulfilling one's self, that's a very good thing to do. And it's a very moral thing to do. Anything that's of benefit to other people is a good thing. What I cannot tolerate is deliberately hurting other people."

And, finally, there is the residual effect of Tom's father, the lawyer-turned-inmate-turned bum. It hangs over him, even though he tried to get the man out of his head many years ago. It is why Tom tries to help people in prison.

"There are way, way too many people in prison, being punished for things that they did that were probably wrong, but the punishment is far in excess of the crime. And to the degree that I can, I help those people. My father was in prison three or four different times. He went to pieces and became a bum. I think anything I can do to avoid that, it's all to the better."

A few days after this conversation, Tom emailed me, saying there was something he wanted to add:

"I've spent most of my life living with women, but only in the last twenty years have I begun to understand a man's moral and ethical responsibility toward women. My job as a man is to do everything in my power to care for and uplift my woman. It's my responsibility to make her happy, give her pleasure, delight her, protect her, and make her feel loved.

"A propos: One way to look at the relationship between a man and a woman is to see sex as the core of the matter. I discovered fairly late in life that the key to successful love-making is to put her pleasure first. If I focus on my pleasure, intercourse becomes a way to relieve my itches. But if

I make her the center of my attention and concentrate on giving her pleasure, love-making becomes ecstasy."

Forty-three

You get further by being nice to people than you do by being a pain in the butt.
Johnny Holliday

Where do values and ethics come from? People who offer such things a place of honor in their lives have to find them somewhere, even where an outsider might not look. Johnny Holliday's childhood was not the stuff of dreams. His parents were alcoholics who could not provide him with the parenting the boy needed. Today he is one of the most respected men in his field and in his community. He helps anyone he can. He has a wonderful family to whom he is devoted. Where did these values come from?

"My values, my ethics, I'm pretty sure they had to come from my parents. Not exactly the perfect upbringing. Not exactly the perfect home to grow up in but I still think they instilled in me the right things to do. I've always tried to do things the right way. I'm sure I have many shortcomings. I do the best that I can. You're not going to win over everybody, but if you can win over the majority of them you're ahead of the game. That's what I've always tried to do. Whether or not I'm successful at it, that's for other people to judge."

Do the right thing. It's a theme with the men in this book. What does that mean to Johnny?

"As far as getting along with people and being honest with people and doing a good job. Being somebody in the workplace that they want to be around because you're not a pain in the butt. I'm sure that I have been many times because I like things to be at the top of the game. If they're not, then that bothers me. I don't think I've set limitations that are too unreasonable. I think everybody should work as hard as I do and do things the right way and move on instead of causing problems. I guess that would be the best way to say it."

His standards are high in every area of his life. In his professional life he works hard, probably harder than most people, even those who see themselves as workaholics. But his drive for the right thing doesn't end there.

"Try to be the right way with your family, your kids, your grandkids, and set a good example for them. Have people say 'He's a pretty good guy and he has a great family, wonderful children, and boy how lucky he is.' People say that about Johnny, that he's a good guy with a wonderful family. And how lucky he is. "True, very true," he says.

"I think there are a lot of families that are disconnected and ours is not. Ours is pretty good, pretty solid. We have laughs all the time. It seems like we're all on the same plateau."

Part Ten

Faith, Religion and Spirituality

God, as Truth, has been for me a treasure beyond price. May He be so to every one of us.
Mahatma Gandhi

Forty-four

I don't know if I believe in God or not.
Tom Glenn

There is no shortage of polls, surveys and studies into faith, or lack of it, in America today. Americans are moving away from mainstream religions such as the Methodist or Presbyterian churches to evangelical congregations or no affiliation at all. The Catholic Church has the largest number of former members. Pew Research found that thirteen per cent of all Americans used to be Catholic. I am one of them. So are some of the men whose lives are being profiled on these pages.

There are many reasons why. As for Catholics, the easy answer is the sex scandals that rocked the Church in recent years, but the research shows that people are leaving the Catholic Church for the same reasons they are leaving the mainline Protestant churches. These faiths just don't meet their needs, spiritually speaking.

Belief in God is also eroding, although nine out of ten of us profess to a belief in either God or a universal spirit. Older people are still more religious than younger Americans, although some surveys put the number at less than half who still have a strong belief in God. Millennials, the twenty-somethings, are overwhelmingly disinterested in mainline religions.

But what about the seventy-somethings, the men in this book? What do they believe? All of them were exposed to mainline religions when they were boys, back when just about everyone went to church, whether they wanted to or not.

I will continue with Tom Glenn, the old spy, linguist, opera buff and author.

"When I was six years old I realized my parents' values were not the ones I wanted and at that point I mentally pulled myself away from them. I thought the values I wanted were in the Catholic Church and I was a very devout Catholic. I went to church every day and often took communion every day, that kind of thing, right up through my teens. I was a deep believer."

He was alone in his deep belief. "My mother never went to church anywhere. My father pretended to be Catholic but he often didn't go to church. He would take me to church, drop me off and say he was going to park the car and come on in. He never showed up. I would come back out and he would be there. I would say, "Where were you?' He would say he looked for me in church but he couldn't find me. Finally, I realized he wasn't coming in at all. I could smell liquor on his breath. He would drop me off at church, go to a bar and come back and pick me up."

As for his budding faith and his search for meaning in his life, "It was a question of doing it myself because nobody was going to do it for me."

As he grew older he dropped out of the Church. It didn't happen overnight. "It was a gradual process. I stayed pretty much a Catholic during my twenties. In my thirties I began to say I don't like what this church is doing and I don't think I want to do this anymore. I gradually moved away from the Church when they condemned homosexuals and when they refused to recognize people who were divorced." One of the contributing factors was the breakup of his first marriage. As a divorced man he was no longer welcome at Mass. “That was fine with me because I didn’t want to be there, anyway.”

His leaving was not easy for him. The Church had provided a moral anchor, a set of rules by which to lead a virtuous life. “If I left the Church I had to decide on my own what was right and wrong and what I was going to do to be virtuous and so on.”

On reflection, he sees a deep goodness in the Catholic Church, even though he has serious questions about some of its moral positions. “The things that I condemn the Catholic Church for are really just a few things. Most of what’s taught is universal goodness and condemning things like murder, hurting others, thievery and so on. So much of what I believe in did, in fact, come from the Catholic Church. Where the Church and I differ are people they condemn and I do not.”

Here he is, years later, facing the same overriding human question. Does God exist?

“I don’t know if I believe in God or not. I do pray at night because I very much want to believe in God but I can’t quite do it. I see no evidence in living, in life.” He pauses. “That’s not quite true. Lately, with this magnificent (spring) weather, I’m just overwhelmed by the beauty of the earth. That makes me think there must have been a God to have created all of this.”

Forty-five

Jesus had the right philosophy of life,
whether he was real or not.
Jared Grantham

In the story of Job, part of the Old Testament of the Bible, God puts Job, a good man, through a series of trials to test his faith. For Job, it's one thing after another, all of them terrible. In the end, God finds Job worthy because he hasn't lost his faith.

Jared Grantham's life has been a series of trials, "shaping experiences," as he calls them. Polio that nearly killed him. The loss of his son Joel. A few years ago he fell down some stairs and broke his neck and was clinically dead for a few minutes. Fortunately, it happened at a medical school and physicians were nearby to save him. His life has been marked by as much suffering as success. Has it shaken his faith? You bet. Does he rail at God and ask, "Why me?"

"I gave that up long ago. That's why I'm an agnostic."

Unlike Job, Jared thought it over and decided it was all just the luck of the draw. "If God was really looking out for me why was he putting so much shit on my shoulders? I gave up on that 'why me?' thing. It's all statistical."

He grew up in the Methodist Church in a small farming town in western Kansas. Faith was a given. Everyone went to church and prayed for rain in the summer and enough moisture over the winter to produce a good wheat crop. Values were built around Biblical lessons. Jared's shaping experiences gave him time to think about the great issues of life.

"I'm not religious anymore. That irritates my wife no end but she understands it. I don't believe in the hereafter. When I'm gone, I'm gone. I don't expect to be up there on a cloud with all of my relatives and that other stuff. My view of that is you do the best you can to make heaven on Earth while you're here. That's what I'm trying to do now with the time I have left."

Issues of mortality are never far away for Jared. As he neared his eightieth birthday he was diagnosed with cancer. We discussed religion a few days before he began chemo-therapy. He was calm about it.

"I was close to death twice. Once when I had polio I was really a sick cookie. I was hallucinating. I saw people who were so real I thought I could touch them. Once I tried to do that and fell out of bed. What I had were these weird hallucinations but I didn't see Jesus, didn't meet God. I didn't do any of that."

As we learned in the section on loss, whatever faith he had ended when his son Joel was killed in a train accident. Then, a few years ago, another "shaping experience."

"When I fell at the library I was turning black, I wasn't breathing. They did external massage on my heart and mouth-to-mouth resuscitation to keep my brain alive. I didn't have the out-of-body supernatural experiences that people talk about."

Jared is a scientist. He believes in what can be proven by scientific means. God, he says, "he, she, or it, has just decided not to spend too much time on me."

He, on the other hand, is spending whatever time he has left pondering his life and writing down his thoughts. "What I'm trying to do in the time I have available is to touch base with as many people in this world that I know and love and affirm them. I am writing my experience down and will probably write a little essay called The Last Shaping Experience." In it, he will explain what he thinks about God.

"God is nature. God is love. God is all these things we cannot measure. Some people call it God. I don't call it God. I just call it life, love."

Forty-six

I believe that the spirit lives on.
Lamont Gibson

Ask a man about his spiritual beliefs and the most likely response you will get is an embarrassed pause. Embarrassed may not be the right word. Considered might be more accurate. Most of the men who were asked this question took time to answer. Only the atheists were quick with their response. It is a sign that the question is very personal and must be weighed against prevailing public opinion or the feelings of parents, teachers, ministers, or others who had religious expectations for the man who, as a boy, was required to go to church.

Lamont Gibson was such a boy. He was exposed to both Catholic and Baptist services. He went to Catholic schools and was an altar boy during the days when the Mass was said in Latin.

Are you a religious man?

Pause. "I wouldn't describe myself as a religious man. I am spiritual. I do believe in God. I believe there is a higher being. I do not go to church. I do feel as though I carry the values of a person who is religious. I do feel it is important to treat people well. I feel it is important to respect people."

He touched on respect in his comments about values and ethics. He believes one should treat others as one would hope to be treated. He passed along this belief to his son. He told the young man that treating people well is more important than success, although being seen as a good person can lead to success in other areas of life. Lamont says his religious or spiritual beliefs today are an accumulation of all that he has learned about life and behavior from his early life to his retirement years.

"I had two very strong religious influences. My mother went to a Baptist church and I went to Catholic schools. There was always religion around me. Those were the days when you wore a suit on Sunday when you went to church."

As a boy his summers were spent with grandparents in Montgomery, Alabama. His grandparents were very religious and took him to Baptist services. "It depended on what church it was and what day it was. Sometimes the services lasted two hours or just one hour, depending on what was happening. Sometimes a Gospel choir would sing."

"I had mixed emotions about the churches. In the Catholic masses there was a strict ceremony, a sequence of events. In the Baptist service you would be exposed to the personal feelings of the minister. The older I got the more critical I became of the ministers who would say things that just weren't true. Some of these ministers had slanted opinions. I attributed it to a lack of education. Catholic priests were required to have a bachelor's degree at a minimum. The emphasis on education in the Catholic Church was impressive and that's why I put my son in Catholic schools."

When did you stop going to church?

"When I left high school. I went into the military. There was no requirement. (laughs) From time to time I would go back, every five or ten years, to check it out. I never hooked on to going to church on a regular basis. I went to church when my son was growing up because I wanted him to be affiliated with a church. Regardless of what he did as an adult, that would be his decision. He would have the choice to accept or not."

Now the big question. Do you believe in an afterlife?

"There are a lot of different definitions of an afterlife. One definition is heaven or hell, that you may rise up or fall down. There's another perception that there is reincarnation, that your spirit lives on here on Earth. There are many perceptions of an afterlife. In some people's minds it doesn't exist, may not exist at all. I believe that the spirit lives on, whether it is in a state of bliss, heaven, or whether it's reincarnated into another person or life form. Just by keeping a positive attitude you are enhancing your spiritual self."

Lamont, like the other men in this book, has come a long way from where he began and he has done it by believing in himself, moving past obstacles, and remaining positive. "You feel good about yourself when you have taken a positive power attitude about things. When things seem to go wrong and yet when you walk away and you look back on it and say it turned out all right, it makes you feel better about yourself when you keep a happy, positive attitude."

Maybe it will carry him into whatever form the afterlife has to offer.

Forty-seven

Is there an afterlife? Beats the hell out of me.
Grady Smith

Let's stay with the Catholic guys in this chapter. Lamont went to Catholic schools. Grady Smith did him one better. He went to seminary to study for the priesthood. It was only the prospect of a celibate life that drove him out. His education taught him about faith, the Church, the great philosophers of Catholisism, and, finally, about himself.

Is he a practicing Catholic?

"No, once I walked away I never went back. I'm talking for four or five decades. Someplace in the swirl of being in the Army and in Vietnam and living in eleven different houses in eight years and a couple of combat tours and that kind of thing kind got left behind. That sounds paradoxical at first because you know the old stereotype is no atheists in foxholes. I'm not sure walking away from an organized religion is atheism. It's a turn away from formality and form and Thou Shalt Not. It's a turning away from that to a more frankly spiritual approach rather than commandments and rituals and 'don't think for yourself, we'll tell you what's right and wrong.'"

What about God. Do you believe in God?

"I do but it's kind of generic. I'm not sure what the hell is out there. I think there's something out there. It's profoundly offensive, at the same time it's very simple to think that the universe has always been there and did not have a cause; that the universe itself, the physicality of it and all of the complex laws it operates on is an uncaused cause. I don't think the universe is the result of a spontaneous crap shoot."

His years in seminary have given him a deep rooting in philosophy and exposure to the great thinkers of Catholicism. "I think it was one of Aquinas' five proofs of the existence of God. Over the years philosophers have attacked each of those and refuted them but it still has validity for me. I don't need to genuflect to a latter day philosopher any more than I need to genuflect to an organized religion. (St. Thomas Aquinas was a 13th Century Catholic philosopher who put forth five logical arguments for the existence of God. They are: The unmoved mover; the first cause; the argument from contingency; the argument from degree; and the theological argument. Aquinas is not light reading.)

"My sense is there is a higher power out there, that there is some kind of cause. That doesn't have to be a Christian deity in the sense that he knows me personally and calls me by name. It could be an abstract compendium of the laws that the universe operates under. That can be a higher power, that can be a deity. I don't know how all that works, if that's the model. Where did all of this come from?"

But humans have spent thousands of years asking two questions: Who or what created us and what happens after we die?

"Beats the hell out of me. That is one of those things that is an adjunct to faith. The classic definition of faith is belief in things not seen. I've never seen an afterlife. I've never seen anybody who came back from an afterlife. I've heard stories. That's right up there with a belief in God. I've never seen one. I've never had a burning bush experience. So what I do is, I act as though there is and if there's isn't, nothing lost, you know. It works much better than to act as if there is not and find out, oh shit, there is."

What about good and evil? Do they exist?

"Yes. Boy, profoundly and yet at the same time at a very simple level good and evil are on the world stage. What reassures me about this good/evil thing is looking at the people I see every day, my neighbors, my friends in recovery. These are the folks that give me heart and make it possible to walk through the day."

Good and evil. Heaven or hell. Love or hate. Peace or war. These are profound questions for a man with the soul of a poet who spent a good portion of his life as a soldier, a man who has seen the worst that humans can do to each other.

"We can have a universe without a deity and still have good and evil. Some people say the universe has a divinity and some people say don't be an idiot. There's still good and evil out there for both sides. Some people say it's not good or evil, just ad hoc decisions day in and day out."

Grady has spent many hours pondering the question of God, creation, the universe, and his role in all that is. "My bottom line on the good/evil question is I sense I have the ability to choose my actions and I can choose actions that harm others or I can choose actions that help them. And that for me is where the good/evil dichotomy lies."

Forty-eight

Mass to me is a chance to go and talk to the man upstairs.
Johnny Holliday

Life-shattering experiences can profoundly affect a man's spiritual life. As we saw with Jared Grantham, his polio, the death of his son, and other "shaping" experiences sapped his belief in God, leaving him a self-described agnostic.

Johnny Holliday has also experienced life-altering events but it drew him closer to God. In 1975 he was nearly killed in a small plane crash. A few years later he nearly bled to death following a surgical procedure. Johnny will detail both events in a later chapter.

My first question for Johnny was, are you a religious man?

"I would say from time to time. I think it bothers me that I'm not more religious. I was after the airplane accident." In the aftermath of the crash he promised God he would be a better man if he lived.

He was not religious as a boy. "The thing for me on Sunday was to be with my buddies and get in a boat and waterski or go to the beach or play ball."

High school got him to attend church, but not necessarily for the right reasons. "I dated a girl who was very religious and the only way to get to first base with her was to go to church with her. I never got to first base with her but I went to church with her. I wasn't even a member of her denomination but I got elected state secretary at their convention.

They had a camp at Ocala National Park and I went up there and got elected secretary." (laughs) His basketball coach got him to attend his church. "He was a Sunday school teacher."

Then he met Mary Clare, the love of his life. She was Catholic. "When we got married it was pretty much Mass every Sunday and when the girls came along she made even more certain that I was going to set an example for the kids."

His work life began to interfere with his attendance at Mass. "Travel problems and so forth. I can't go because I've got games in different cities and I'm tired. That's no excuse but it's an excuse that I use."

For a period of time he slacked off and slept in. "Mary Clare goes by herself and that's not good. After the airplane accident I came full circle again, realizing how lucky I was. You make a promise to the man upstairs, I'm going to do this, I'm going to do that. Its lasts awhile and then it's back to the old routine again. Then when the girls got married you start again by going back. Mass to me is a chance to just go and talk to the man upstairs, myself. I'm always apologizing. I'd like to be nicer. I'd like to be this or that. I'm sorry for this or I'm sorry for that. And whether you're forgiven or not is anybody's guess. You never know until that final bell is rung."

Johnny believes in God.

"I do. I do. I don't know what's up there. I think about it sometimes. I believed when I had that accident that I was here for a reason. I very easily could have been taken in 1975 with that plane crash, it could have gone the other way. Or thirteen years ago when I had the internal hemorrhaging thing going on that put me in the hospital for thirty days. That was really close, probably closer than the plane crash. Both of them I got through and there must have been a reason why I got through those things."

Johnny is deep spiritual thinker. He sees where he's been and he knows where he is now and all that he has accomplished. He feels blessed. He cherishes his time alone with his belief.

"The biggest time for me is when I'm in my car. I turn the radio off and it's just me and I do a lot of talking to the man upstairs. It's a cleansing thing for me. I don't know. That's the way I kind of work my life into religion. I tell my mom and dad how much I love them." Here he becomes emotional in much the way he did when he discussed his parents in an earlier chapter. Johnny is a man who travels in a special world of accomplishment and gratitude.

Forty-nine

I don't condemn religion.
Jim King

I will conclude this section with the two avowed atheists in the group, our "Jims," King and Bohannon. Both men grew up going to church and both men now soundly reject any belief in an intelligent being who controls the universe. I will begin with Jim King.

Did you ever believe in God?

"As a child, of course. You believe what your parents tell you. Somewhere around fourteen or fifteen I read a book, something about the reality of Jesus as a person, and he may have been a I won't say fake but he believed he was the messiah but he really wasn't, and it got me to thinking. I started analyzing and looked at the Bible and read some of it. And on my own terms I determined that this was basically a fable. If you're a good kid you will get your toys. That's to me what religion was. If you're a good boy and do what they say you will go to heaven. I figured that out for myself and what I think is true. So no, I don't believe in God."

But that does not mean that Jim doesn't believe in anything or right and wrong. "I believe in morality because it's necessary for society. Without it we're just a bunch of apes doing what we want when we want when we want to. The only thing we care about is ourselves and we can't do that and have a family or any kind of society."

So, do you believe that when it's over, it's really over?

"Pretty much, yes."

Several men have said the issues of right and wrong they were exposed to in the churches of their boyhood carried over into their adults lives, whether they still believe in God or not. Issues such as love and charity.

"I don't condemn religion. I think if people are religious and they act in that manner in their daily lives that is a good thing and I applaud them for doing that. I think religion has value for many people. It gives them comfort. I'm all for that if they're happy, if it helps them through the day and makes them a better person. I'm all for that. I believe in humanity. I believe in laws. I believe in the things that keep us together as a group. I don't think there is somebody watching my every move and who will condemn me after I'm dead."

###

Jim Bohannon shares similar beliefs. He went to church as a boy and grew away from it as an adult. He believes in the rational mind and says there is no evidence of God anywhere. I asked him whether he thinks there is a difference between religion and spirituality; a higher being as opposed to religious dogma?

"I find it difficult to separate them entirely. I don't know precisely what is spiritualism outside religion. I guess the short answer would be I just haven't seen any evidence to that effect. There may well be some guiding intelligence but we have no evidence of it. We only have one universe that we know about. If we had seventeen universes and thirteen of them were guided in this way by some super intelligence that would be an empirical basis for arriving at that conclusion. But we don't know much about this universe. For all we know we could be a failed science fair experiment in the fifth dimension. We don't know what this universe is. I try not to bother myself that much with things about which I know little and can do little."

Bohannon concedes that many of his core values began in church as a boy, things such as kindness and helping others. He acknowledges that much good has been done in the name of religion and appears to believe it outweighs the bad, such as the inquisition or ISIS.

Is it possible to believe in God without being religious?

"I think so. It's possible to have the former without subscribing to the latter. This is something I think about very little."

He does have one beef with religion, which he expressed after I prompted him.

"The biggest beef would be this: the assertion that 'I want to believe something therefore I am going to.' That just flies in the face of my logical mind. It's an assault on the whole concept of reasonable thinking."

Part Eleven

Aging

Age, with his stealing steps,
Hath clawed me in his clutch.
Hamlet

Fifty

I'm operating at a 30 per cent level of a normal person my age.
Jared Grantham

The old joke about life is, you'll never get out alive. But with luck you'll be old when the end comes. Unfortunately, that involves actually getting old and all that it means. The hard reality is that aging cannot be prevented, no matter what the health gurus tell us about what to eat, think, or breathe. As each year passes, we age. Our hearts lose capacity, our brains shrink, our eyesight diminishes, our motor skills deteriorate and our balance is not what it once was. These are just the highlights. I won't get into the sagging skin, thinning hair and various organs that act like parts in old cars that need to go to the shop.

It is also true that not everyone ages the same. We all have heard the stories about the ninety-five year old man who smokes a pack of cigarettes a day, washed down with a fifth of bourbon, fathers children, and runs marathons every weekend. If that guy exists, he's a freak of nature. Heavy smokers tend to get culled from the herd earlier than non-smokers. So, too, heavy drinkers and guys who are morbidly obese. The rest of us just watch our necks wrinkle.

There are things we can do to make life more interesting and even fun as we slowly watch the sun set. Keeping busy with things that involve both mind and body can keep us healthy, or maybe just healthier, than the guy who sits in his recliner morning 'til night watching television and eating ice cream.

I will begin this part with Jared Grantham, the medical researcher whose physical limitations caused by childhood polio keep him from doing what other men his age can do, even if they choose not to. His body doesn't allow much room for activity, so he lives in his mind.

"I'm different from ninety-nine per cent of those who age. I'm a scholar. My definition of a scholar is a person who is never satisfied with what they know. You're always trying to learn something new. The vast majority of those who are aging have stopped growing. Many are content to sit on the front porch and rock, maybe listen to the Royals. Or they eat three meals a day and get unhappy because they're getting old and they can't do what they used to do. They're just kind of lost souls. I'm not like that."

He's not like that for many reasons. "I had an evaluation ten years ago and I rated thirty per-cent whole. I'm operating at a thirty per-cent level of a person my age." The thirty per-cent is physical ability, not mental. "So that's what I've got to work with. I think my brain is pretty close to ninety, ninety-five or one-hundred per cent. As long as that's there it kind of overrides all of these other infirmities. You find that when you're disabled you end up developing all kinds of ways to get around little problems, little tools that you have. You invest a little time in making it easier for yourself."

Maybe that's the key, not only for Jared, but for all of us. Maybe we should all spend a little time making it easier for ourselves. We can all find ways to overcome our encroaching infirmities by eating right, getting enough sleep, getting some exercise, and getting over the idea that aging is something that is being inflicted on us. We're the lucky ones, we who get old. We can appreciate that it's a gift, not an affliction. We can think of all those we knew when we were young who don't have the luxury of complaining about how old they are.

Fifty-one

There's nothing nagging me more than saying,
Boy are you ever old.
Jim Bohannon

With luck, everyone will one day wake up, look in the mirror, and see an old person. It sneaks up, one day at a time, over decades. We go through life marking little milestones, some good, some not so good, and then, there it is, the white hair, what's left of it.

Jim Bohannon has been reflecting on these milestones, what he calls "the flipping over of digits on my lifetime odometer." What moments were really a big deal? "Well, sixteen, when I got my driver's license, which I did on the first day I was eligible, and managed to drive by the homes of all my friends who were still on their bicycles. That was a big day."

Five years later, another landmark. "Twenty-one. I could drive and I could vote. Both of them were quite important to me at that time."

So sixteen and twenty-one, two important milestones, digit-turnings, in Jim's life. Drive, drink, vote. The landmarks that allowed him entry into the world of adult privilege. These are birthdays that gave him something he wanted, something that allowed him to move away from the restrictions of childhood. After those two birthdays, the excitement died down.

"Thirty? Eh. Not really, putting through life. Forty? Same thing, putting through life. Fifty? We're getting to the age that upsets some people. Fifty, I remember nothing about. Actually, it was my fiftieth birthday when I stopped smoking. That's the only thing I remember about that birthday. It's like we often do in life. We point at that which we, for arbitrary reasons, say that's what we'll change."

"Sixty? My wife threw a wonderful birthday party for me on my sixtieth birthday, had a whole slew of friends. We rented a hotel meeting room. There were a lot of people there. I remember thinking it's a pretty big deal. Here I am five years away from Social Security. I didn't feel bad about it. I was glad to see everybody. It was particularly charming because she had wanted it to be a roast and everybody wound up saying these wonderful things about me. It sounded like the Mother Theresa roast. After that, well you know, sixty-five. I started getting my AFTRA pension, the broadcasters union pension. Social Security at sixty-six." On to his eighth decade. "Seventy? Just another birthday, really. And those were the high points."

Here he is, seventy-two at this writing, no longer the skinny kid with the horn-rimmed glasses. It doesn't bother him that the kid is long gone. "Aging hasn't been that big a deal to me. I haven't felt old. I don't have physical ailments. My mind isn't slipping. I'm pretty sure of that because I have a job where management would not be shy about telling me."

Older men will often say they feel fine, even good on some days. Our bodies are in need of repair here and there but overall, we're happy to be in this side of the grass. So it is with Jim.

"Physically, I'm not as fast as I used to be. I'm probably as strong as I ever was. I'm overweight and I don't take care of myself as I should. The doctors say I'm in good shape. There's nothing nagging me and saying, Boy are you ever old. I have a white beard and the hair on top of my head is disappearing. Other than that, as Bob Green, the writer, put it when he was asked what he felt like when he turned sixty-five and he said, 'I feel like a teenager who's been in a fight.'"

Fifty-two

The idea that maybe I will get sick and won't be able to write is the worst thing I can think of.
Tom Glenn

It is every old person's nightmare. The prospect that we will become like the folks in the nursing homes, sitting around in wheelchairs in a television room, unable to care for ourselves, dependent on others, and slowly rotting away. That may be one reason why older people are always pushing themselves and going for walks or playing tennis and responding to TV ads that show white-haired people water skiing.

It's Tom Glenn's nightmare. He thinks about it more than he wants to. Lung cancer scared him into taking a look at his physical self and wondering about the future.

Do you see yourself as an old man?

"No, oddly enough. I probably should but I don't."

At what point did you no longer see yourself as a young man?

"I don't know that I ever did that. I do have mental discussions with myself about looking at myself, particularly after the cancer, and seeing my body half destroyed. But somehow I don't feel that way. I still feel like I'm a man who can go out and get things done, things like working on the deck. I thoroughly enjoy every minute of it, by the way."

Despite his time spent in life-threatening situations as an intelligence operative, Tom, like Jared Grantham, is a man who lives in his head. He risked his body in combat situations and came close to losing it many times, but he survives with his thoughts and his need to write them down. Unlike a construction worker who would notice the slow degeneration of his ability to use his body as a tool, Tom's tool, his mind, is sharp as ever and has not given him a reason to think of himself as old.

"I think to myself I really am an old man but I don't feel like it. It just doesn't feel like I'm an old person. I don't remember thinking I'm not young anymore. I guess my mental attitude is I'm probably just as young as I ever was."

Cancer forced Tom to face the hard truth that all things must pass, even men. "I don't deal with it well. The prospect of death really bothers me. I think about it a lot this year because I was so close. I don't want my life to end. I don't want to die. I comfort myself by saying, Tom, it's universal, everybody dies. So I tell myself I will make the very best use of the time I have and I will work very hard to stay as healthy as I can so that I will live to be past one-hundred and I will be working right up to the end and then maybe I will be peaceful and I can say I did a good job and I can go now."

It's the fantasy that's common among older people: Happily doing what we love and suddenly, painlessly, we fall over dead. No long slide down to the abyss. "I could accept the idea that I would be charging straight ahead and one day I will fall over and that would be the end. I could live with that. (We both got a big laugh out of that line.) The idea that it might be slow and agonizing and go on for years where I can't get anything done and I might be living in a nursing home or something like that just gives me the chills."

Fifty-three

It's very useful to see ourselves the way other people in different age contexts see us.
Grady Smith

Getting older is a pain in the ass, let's face it. Despite the cheery television ads about how great it is to be an active older person, how much golf we can play or how many blue pills we can swallow to invigorate our sex lives, we will never be twenty-five again. Things happen to the human body as it ages and there's really not much that can be done about it. One day at a time, every day of our lives, we get older. Period. The secret, then, if it is a secret, is to do what we must to be as healthy as we can for as long as we can.

Grady Smith, retired military officer and theater scholar, is an example of someone making the best of it.

"Well, it's true, you reach a certain age and your life is structured around visits to doctors' offices. So, that's kind of aging. But you see if you're proactive on the medical side you don't have lots of time to correct physical maladies and if we don't have lots of down time we can, in fact, participate in life as fully as our bodies and our minds and our emotions and our spirit let us do that."

When we're young we don't really think about aging. We think our middle aged parents are old and our grandparents were born before modern life. There comes a day when it dawns on us that we are now the older ones. The dreaded middle age of bellies and the first gray hair. For Grady, middle age arrived in the form of a fresh-faced cop.

"I never noticed it happening. I was just living, rup, rup, rup, just going along. Katy was transferred to St. Louis and we were mid to late forties and we came back, I must have been in my early or mid-fifties and we drove back. It was snowing. We were taking it carefully along this street and we stopped. This very, very young Fairfax County police officer came over as we were stopped in traffic and he asked, 'Are you all right, sir?' I thought, I am not only middle aged but I'm quivering on the verge of the next plateau. The cop looked like he might have just got out of high school. I thought, this is how he reacted to me."

Grady thinks it's good to take a step back and look at ourselves through the eyes of others. "It's very useful in this thing to see ourselves the way other people in different age contexts see us. As long as we don't let that determine our actions, our desires, our life goals, our year goals. Okay, I can be that age and still maintain what I want to do."

How's his health?

"Not bad. I kicked booze thirty-eight years ago, that was a big one, that's why I'm still around, I'm convinced of it. In 2008 I had prostate cancer. I'm cured of it, according to my urologist. I've got a pacemaker as of 2013. My cardiologist went from suggesting to directing and now he's getting shrill so I'm losing some weight and that's going to add about fifty-thousand miles to the chassis, whatever fifty-thousand miles means in terms of calendar years."

That's the physical side of aging, the parts that need to be fixed or replaced. There's another side to staying alive in our seventies and eighties. "I gotta tell you one of the things that really helps my physical health is not being isolated and getting out and being with people. My wife and I go to forty-five or fifty plays a year. We get together with family and also with friends of mine in recovery." He's had cataract surgery and was amazed to find that the world is in vivid, living color. With his cataracts the world had become a kind of grey sepia.

Of course, the reality of aging is never far away, no matter where he goes. "These young folks will hold the door open for us when we go into the theater or the hotel. Do I look that feeble? (laughs) My god, I didn't feel rickety until they held the door open for me."

Fifty-four

If I over-exert myself am I going to go down and pass out?
Johnny Holliday

Johnny Holliday is like Dick Clark, forever energized, youthful, a voice that sounds like it did when he was twenty-five. Part of that is lifestyle, part of it is attitude, some of it is good genes, and part of it is his belief that nothing is really impossible, even at age seventy-eight.

"I think I can still probably do anything I did when I was young right now. I honestly believe I can still hit a ball, I can still make a layup, I can throw the ball(pause) I can't throw the ball because of a bad shoulder. (laughs) If I had the time to play I would probably still be playing in a seventh-and-over basketball league. I played in sixty-and-over and sixty-five-and-over. And the only thing that concerns me now is the silent heart attack I had several years ago. Part of my heart is not working. Instead of one-hundred per cent it's probably ninety per-cent or eighty-eight per cent. They put a defibrillator in after I had that hemorrhaging thing and that is always in the back of my mind and concerns me. If I over exert myself am I going to go down and pass out or is that thing going to go off?"

From April to October Johnny works almost every day doing the pre- and post-game shows for the Washington Nationals baseball team. In the fall and winter he does play-by-play for the University of Maryland football and basketball teams. He also acts as master of ceremonies for awards banquets and other events.

Sports has always been important to him and he measures his aging by how well he can still play. "It never bothered me getting older. I could still throw a ball and run, not as fast, but I never really thought that I would ever lose the ability to play ball. I know I have but I think it's all in your mind that you can still play if you want to. Maybe not as good but you can still play and have fun."

There are telltale signs that things are not quite where they were years ago. "I was out pitching to one of my grand-daughters the other day. I realized that maybe the reflexes aren't there. She's eight years old, hit a line drive and almost took my head off. I realized that maybe I should move back a little." (laughs)

In the fall of 2016 Johnny celebrated his sixtieth year in broadcasting. Sixty years is a long time to do anything. It's an extraordinarily long time to do it well. Who does he see when he looks in the mirror? How much of the young hot-shot disc jockey is still there?

"I think I see somebody who's aged pretty gracefully. The hair is a little different. The weight is a little more than when I was twenty-one. But I think the wisdom is more than ever. I haven't lost any of that stuff. I haven't lost the desire to work, to create, to respond, to be at the top of my game. I think it's all still there. So when I look in the mirror I think I might look a little younger than seventy-eight. I don't know, that's what I see."

There have been studies that show a link between longevity and work; the longer we work, the longer we live. If so, Johnny will live a very long time, despite his various ailments.

Doing live television every day requires him to remain sharp. "Working on TV with the Nationals, you're around ballplayers, you're interviewing, you're reacting, you're thinking on your feet. You follow instructions from producer John Harvey talking in my ear at the same time Ray (Knight, a former player) is talking to me from one side. I'm trying to decipher what he's saying, what the producer is saying and following what the camera is saying with countdowns. I can still put it all together." Ray Knight, his broadcast partner, was Most Valuable Player of the 1986 World Series. He is a former manager of the Cincinnati Reds and third baseman for the New York Mets.

Doing play-by-play for Maryland requires him to memorize lineups and follow the game in real time for radio listeners. It requires a fast mind and a gift for description. It requires him to use his brain and it may have kept his brain young. "I think it's still there. If it starts to go I'm hoping I'm the first one to know it."

Fifty-five

You get tired fast, you sleep longer.
Jim King

Jim King knew he was getting older when he couldn't recover from shift changes as a police officer. He was around forty at the time. He went back into uniform after serving as a detective and found himself back on the streets, working rotating shifts.

"As a detective I didn't do that many midnight shifts. When I went back on the road as a uniform I had to do that constant shift change. It just killed me. It was so hard to work all night, sleep all day, and get up raring to go in the evening again. It took me days to readjust and then I was changing shifts again. It was like constant jet lag. My mind was good but my body just wasn't recovering. It was telling me I can't do this anymore. That's why police officers and fire fighters retire early."

When did middle age begin for you?

"Somewhere in my mid-forties. I was still pretty good at thirty-five but by forty-five I was beginning to slow down and it took longer to recover from aches and pains."

At what age did you think you were an old man?

"Probably in my mid-sixties. I couldn't run fast anymore, I was not as agile, I had heart troubles, high blood pressure, you're not as strong as you use to be. You can't do the things you used to do. Instead of raking leaves all day long, after an hour or two or less you have to sit down and say let me take a break here. You get tired fast, you sleep longer. It takes me longer in the morning to wake up and get the engine running."

How's your health?

"Pretty good. I've been a smoker all my life. I'm totally addicted to smoking. That's the reason in the early eighties I went to a pipe. At least with a pipe I don't inhale as much and it makes me look intelligent." (laughs)

An aging body is different from a young body and it's more than just wrinkles and gray hair. "One of the things I hate the most nowadays is I don't have as much fat under my skin and I bruise. I look down and I have a bruise and I don't even remember what I did to get the bruise. I just bump my hand against a table or something and I've got a bruise that looks like hell."

Most young people fear aging because of what it looks like on the outside. Jim says these things are nothing to be feared. "We have a youth-oriented society. Everybody wants to look young, dye their hair. They don't want to have gray hair and they don't want to have saggy skin and I get that. But if you're lucky, some day you will have sagging skin and gray hair and that means you've lived a long time. That's the whole thing about eating right and exercising, so you can live longer and better. Those of us who have hit our seventies have accomplished that, knowingly or not."

Okay, maybe there a bit of tongue in cheek to his "eating right and exercising" words.

"I drink, I smoke, I chase wild women, I keep late hours and I'm still here." (laughs) "I guess it's the luck of the draw."

Fifty-six

I dealt with it by dancing
Lamont Gibson

Every man profiled on these pages is dealing with an aging body. The mirror doesn't lie. Nor does the doctor who breaks the news about high blood pressure, heart disease, or some other age-related physical ailment.

Lamont Gibson has managed to avoid most of those problems but he admits the clock is ticking.

"I didn't want to admit it. I didn't want to accept it. I dealt with it by dancing and exercising and finding the things that made me happy and just doing them," he says.

He knows he needs to take care of himself to put off the inevitable. "I've taken a strong and serious effort to watch out for it. I go to a military base and make sure I eat a good lunch. I exercise. I average two or three miles a day walking.

What physical limitations do you have now that you didn't have when you were young?

"I'm very, very lucky. I just can't do things as long as I could when I was younger but I can do it all. I can almost palm the floor. I can damn near do a split. I can walk four or five miles. I do line dancing. I don't have high blood pressure, the cholesterol and the various illnesses that come with age, they haven't hit me hard at all. I'm in good health. I'm retired Air Force and I can go to any military hospital and once a year I get a total physical exam. I don't have to take any pills except medication for stomach acid. I got that from the jobs I had."

When you look at yourself in the mirror is there part of you that stills sees a young man?

“No. (laughs) I wish I could. Unfortunately, not. People tell me I look at least ten years younger than I am, but I don’t see a young man. I have a full head of hair. I don’t look as old as I am. I see the reality of who I am. I’m over seventy. My son’s mother died younger than I am. My friends have had strokes. Death is more prevalent than it was before.”

Death. There it is. It’s the subject of jokes among older people. “I could keel over at any minute.” We say it with humor and hope the Grim Reaper isn’t listening. We know it’s coming. It comes for everyone, every last human being.

“I fear death,” Lamont says. “I know it’s inevitable. I’m going to die. I know I’m going to grow old and die. I don’t want to die. I don’t want to die before one hundred. I do everything I can to live to be a hundred.”

Part Twelve

Mortality

When you reach the end of your rope,
tie a knot in it and hang on.
Franklin D. Roosevelt

Fifty-seven

I want to die with a smile on my face.
Lamont Gibson

Wikipedia defines "mortality" as the state of being mortal, or susceptible to death, the opposite of immortality. The men on these pages are aware that they are not immortal. Some have a stated goal of living to be one-hundred. Some have serious health issues, others admit they're overweight. Others concede they have not taken very good care of themselves. For every septuagenarian the issue of mortality is lurking, whether near or not-so-near.

How do they deal with it?

For Lamont Gibson, it's a practical matter marinated in good times. "You know, I make sure I have a will and my papers in order so when I do pass my son will know where everything is. I have a very good insurance policy so he won't have to worry about the funeral. I prepare for death. I know it's coming."

That said, he moves on to other things. "I recognize that I will die. I recognize that I should enjoy life. I do the things that make me happy. I do the things that are nice things."

He has a very generous retirement income that gives him the freedom to do pretty much what he wants to do. He has two Mercedes and a Jaguar. "I own five houses. I try to live as well as I can to enjoy life. I know it's going be over." Two of his properties are Florida condos that he rents out with staggered leases, so every year or so he travels to Florida to stay in the one that a renter is leaving. He goes on two cruises a year. He lives in a four-thousand square foot suburban home outside Washington. He watches a big screen television.

"I party. I dance. I enjoy going out and listening to live music. I travel. I treat work likes drugs, I just say no." (Laughs)

In his work he had positions as an equal employment opportunity officer and in military intelligence as an Air Force officer. He still gets offers to return to intelligence work. "I just say no," he says. "I would rather wake up and chill and maybe play a little basketball or go down to the basement to shoot pool."

His health is good. He is in better health than some of the other men being profiled here.

But nature always takes its course. Lamont would like to live to be one-hundred but he acknowledges his feelings might change if his health deteriorates to a state where he can no longer enjoy life or care for himself.

"I want to die with a smile on my face because I was having fun. No one wants to die suffering."

Fifty-eight

I firmly believe that I will live to be a hundred.
Tom Glenn

Any man in his seventies who cares to look in the mirror in the morning can sense the dark shadow of mortality in the background. It's not just the sagging skin and flagging vitality. It's the numbers. The shadow may not be near but it's lurking. A man who has managed to live to age seventy-five and is still relatively healthy, given the normal ailments of age, can expect to live another ten years. The good news is the longer one lives, the longer one can expect to live. But, as the saying goes, all good things come to an end and the end must be pondered, if not prepared for.

Tom Glenn is a man who has stared death in the face many times and has been convinced, many times, that his end was near. The latest such moment was while I was interviewing him for this book. He was diagnosed with lung cancer, underwent surgery, chemotherapy and radiation. The treatment was successful but it left him weak for months and nearly unable to care for himself, a condition that is his worst nightmare.

Does he see death as a loss?

"Not in the sense that I think you're using the term. When I think about dying, and I've thought a lot about that since the cancer hit, then I have great sorrow over the things that I will lose: The people in my life, my children, the pleasures of sitting down at the computer and writing, beautiful music, playing the piano. All that stuff gives me pleasure. The thought that I will lose all that can make me cry."

When you ponder mortality, is that what comes to mind?

"Yeah. And the other part of pondering mortality is having come very close to death with the cancer. I think, God, I hope it's not like that. I hope it's not this business of lying there and not being able to think and not being able to function; not being able to understand who's talking to you and gradually going down, down and down until there's nothing left. I really hope it's not like that. I hope I will be working one day and fall over dead in an instant."

This feeling of loss and dread is new to Tom. As a young man working as an intelligence agent during the Vietnam War he came close to death many times.

"I saw it very differently. I knew I might be killed and I was in mortal danger and people standing next to me were killed and I knew it was a very real possibility. Then I just accepted it as just how it is and I will do the very best I can to avoid dying. If I can't, well, I can't. That's just all there is to it. It seemed cut and dried to me. Now it doesn't feel like that. Now it feels like it's going to be a long, slow degradation. And having come close to that with the cancer I think, God, I don't want to go through that again. I don't want to look forward to that slow ebbing away and I'm more and more inept. I think it's the ineptitude that frightens me. Back in my days in war ineptitude was just not a problem."

Are your feelings about this stronger about the ineptitude or the loss? When you were younger you had more to lose than you do now. You would have lost the rest of your life and all that has happened to you since then. Did you think about that in Vietnam?

"No. I never thought about the rest of my life, I only thought will I still be here in the morning or will I survive this battle and now I do. Now I am firmly determined that I'm going to live to be a hundred and be competent right to the end because I have so many things I want to do. The sense of loss when I was in my thirties, I was thirty-eight when Saigon fell, almost didn't exist. I never thought about those things. I did think about my children and I thought it would be horrible if they had to grow up without a father. That was their loss, not my loss. Now it's very clear to me what the loss will be."

These days Tom is sometimes overtaken with guilt. Not about what he has done, but how and why he survived the war and so many others did not. It is a common feeling among people who have survived war and other bloody disasters.

"A number of times during the Vietnam War, especially at the end, when I was in Saigon, I thought I'm not going to survive, I'm not going to make it. They were shelling and all it took was one direct hit and it would have been the end of me. I wrote a letter to one of my neighbors and said I'm probably not going to make it and please do your best to take care of my wife and children."

Tom suffers from what he calls PTSI, preferring the word "injury" to "disorder." Its central image for him is something he can only now talk about and it happened during the battle of Dak To in late 1967. It was fierce. Nearly four-hundred Americans were killed and nearly fifteen-hundred were wounded. Tom was in the thick of it. He thought he would never make it out, but he did.

"The guy standing next to me was hit by machinegun fire that almost ripped off his head. And he died horribly and he died in agony and I wasn't hit. We were shoulder to shoulder. Why him? I was undercover. I was dressed as a Marine. Nobody could tell the difference, certainly not the enemy, certainly not the man on the machinegun."

Guilt is a serious issue for Tom. He writes about the horrors that war can inflict on the psyche in his books. For him, there is nothing worse than war's toll on the human soul. "It's for that reason that I want the American people to know how ghastly war is. How unspeakably gruesome combat is. Less than one per cent of us are in the military. We make decisions that are so wrong because we don't understand."

Fifty-nine

I like life, Larry.
Grady Smith

There are as many ways to be born again as there are ways to die. Most of us in our later years focus on the dying part, when we think about it at all. Grady Smith was given life twice. The first time was his birth. The second time was when he put down his last glass of booze and began to live a sober life.

"It was a kind of rebirth. I think there's a rearrangement of psychic furniture when a real alcoholic is finally able to put on the brakes and put down the glass and face life on life's terms."

Grady had been sober for thirty-eight years when we had this conversation. He still recalled the new life sobriety offered him. He still appreciated the sweetness of it.

"It was almost like getting new lenses. Once the fog lifts and the atmosphere clears life looks different. I had my last glass of booze in November. I vividly remember my first spring. It was all colors and sweet odors and landscapes to kill for."

So now, with his eightieth birthday only two years away, does he think about what may lie ahead?

"Yes, from time to time. I haven't gotten deeply morose or anything nor have I gotten around to the eternal punishment thing or the eternal reward thing. I think that's part of the formal religion apparatus. It may very well be."

Grady is well-travelled and well-read. His early years in seminary gave him an education in Christian thought but he's also looked at Eastern religions for guidance on values and what lies behind this life.

"You know I have dabbled in my personal reading on the Buddhist side and those other faiths that deal with reincarnation. I don't know if we come back around or not. I have no recollection of a previous life so I can't make an educated guess on that. I don't know if there is or not."

Grady says he wants to wait until he has reason to think he's facing the end before he gives it much thought. "I reserve the right to get very preoccupied once I know the name of whatever it is that will kill me. That changes the game right there. Right now I'm thinking about it as a kind of taking a pulse on this issue. The last time I checked, I frankly did not know whether there was an afterlife or not and that did not worry me."

When it comes will it be with a sense of loss or relief?

"When I take a broad view of the world or our country, I'm not going to be sad to say goodbye. When I think about art and literature and theater, the harvest of the human mind and spirit and then when I think about family, friends and activities, just doing, yes, it makes me sad."

Sixty

When it happens, it happens.
Jim Bohannon

There it is in the mirror. Mortality looking back. "Wrinkly," to use Jim's word. We go through life watching old people die and then one day we realize we are the old people. "You expect old people to die," he said. "I vaguely remember my two grandparents dying. I was in grade school. Old people die. You get wrinkly and bent over and you die."

It is the product of being alive, this wrinkly thing. It waits for every generation. "My parents became wrinkly and bent over and they died. Now, son of a bitch, my people, my cool 1960s Beatle-loving, Elvis-loving people, yeah, we're dying. One fifth of my high school graduation class, twenty per cent of that class, is dead." There were one-hundred-seventy-seven people in the class.

"To be honest with you, I have a weekly ritual. Every Thursday I go to the Lebanon, Missouri, the Lebanon Daily Record obituary page and I print it out. My wife and I read the names of what we call dead Lebanese. In a given month we will probably know one or two people. They are increasingly our peers. I'm starting to hear the term 'natural causes' entirely too much and it's referring to friends of mine. I never saw the point of dwelling on it. When it happens, it happens."

Jim is not a believer. He doesn't believe in God nor does he believe in an afterlife. What does he think happens when a person dies?

"Nothing. Your consciousness is a collection of chemicals between your ears. When that is no longer provided with power and nourishment and energy with blood, it just simply loses the capacity to retain that information and you as an entity and all of your support systems, our pancreas and your toenails and all of that die. Am I dead certain of that? No. I certainly see no evidence of the contrary."

But that does not mean that Jim sees life entirely as a chemical reaction. His consciousness, his emotions, the things he cherishes about being alive, will one day be gone.

"I'm sure I'll miss it. I have a very good life. There are many people, I'm sure, for whom death is merciful, but not for me. I've been very fortunate. Life has been better for me than I deserve. I had not planned that well nor executed that well. It just worked out really well."

There are many men whose final years are spent in regret and even resentment. They blame themselves or others for setbacks or failures or lost love or fortune. Not Jim. "I certainly won't feel cheated. I've had more than my share of recognition, of honors, of, frankly, money. I've been well paid and I'm not sure that's necessarily justified. I've had a good run and I would have no complaints if I were told tomorrow I had horrible stage four pancreatic cancer. I wouldn't like the dying part but to sit back and say 'Woe is me, life is unfair,' how can I say that? My lord, I've had a wonderful life. The only thing I have to whine about is I don't have anything to whine about." (laughs)

Sixty-one.

I can't complain, I'm good to go.
Jim King

There is a certain amount of clock-ticking that accompanies old age. It's the marking of days and the nagging suspicion that mortality is following you around. Most of us have some physical issue we didn't have when we were young. High blood pressure. Weird heartbeats. Sore knees. So when our bodies make themselves known we consider the possibilities. Take Jim King, for instance.

"Every time I get one of my little heart tremors of something, I ask 'Is this the big one?'" (laughs) He offers a rhetorical shrug. "I don't worry about it. It's one of those things, it's gonna happen."

People of faith say they look forward to it, to an afterlife of happiness and joy. Not Jim. "I'm an atheist, I don't believe in an afterlife. The only thing I worry about is how it's going to happen. I'd rather have a heart attack than die slowly of cancer." You will recall that Jim's wife and little girl died of cancer.

He has a little joke to promote his heart attack. "I always say every Big Mac is an investment in the future. If you build up enough of that stuff you're going to go quick. That's my concern. I would much rather have a major heart attack and turn off the switch, like my father did. He just closed his eyes and didn't wake up."

Jim's great grandfather suffered from cancer during a time in which pain killers were not very effective. He killed himself at age ninety-two when the pain became unbearable. "He was an old blacksmith, a carpenter and blacksmith.

He just finally sat on his front porch on his rocking chair one day and pulled out the old .45 and put it to his head." Not an end Jim foresees for himself. When the end comes and life is over, will you miss it?

"No, not at all. Of course, when you're dead, you're dead, there's no afterlife. You won't be anything. It's just like being asleep. Do you miss being awake when you're asleep? No."

He pauses and reflects on the question. "I think I have lived my life fairly well, certainly not perfect. I've always tried to be as honest and as nice as I could be. There are times in everybody's life when you can't be nice and you can't be honest but I've tried to be a nice guy, basically, an honorable person. I don't have too many regrets."

Jim served in the Navy and later as a police officer. He has faced death before but mortality is a very different issue to the young. "I was scared in the Navy when things would happen. Planes would land and explode and you're close by or in the police department when shots were fired and you're running around. That part of my brain turns off in that I never lost rational thought at any time and fear never overcame me. I was very fortunate in having the mindset to do what I was supposed to do in a tense situation."

But this is different. Age is not a tense situation that can be managed with a cool head. It's a time of reflection if life still offers such moments. "I'm sitting here in a house I can afford to pay the monthly on. It's a beautiful summer day with birds singing. I've had a good life. I've had a good family. I've had a good retirement. I can't bitch. Compared to what other people are going through with a life of misery, I've been very, very fortunate in my life. I can't complain. I'm good to go."

Part Thirteen

The Plane Crash

It is necessary to help others, not only
in our prayers, but in our daily lives.
Dalai Lama

Sixty-two

I said we have some things we'd like to give you.
Johnny Holliday

It's one thing to see the shadow of mortality, it is quite another to have it pass over you. For Johnny Holliday, the shadow passed over him twice. Once while he was on a mission of mercy, the second caused by a reaction to medication. Both times he was near death. In the second, a vivid dream of the dead calling to him gave him renewed faith in God and a commitment to be a better man.

Johnny survived a plane crash in 1975 as he was taking relief supplies to a survivor of a natural disaster in Virginia.

"I read in the paper about a ninety-year-old woman who was a survivor in the town of Lovingston." In late 1969 Hurricane Camille moved north and west from the Atlantic and dumped torrential rains on parts of Virginia. Lovingston is the county seat of Nelson County, some two-hundred miles inland. Some parts of the county received forty inches of rain in eight hours. Entire families were wiped out. The *Washington Post's* Ken Ringle wrote a story about an old woman who lived on the mountain and had survived the floods of 1969 and later. The woman was Dora Morris, nearly ninety and living in a slightly ramshackle house her grandfather had built in 1849.

"The story that Ken Ringle wrote was in December of 1974, just before Christmas. There was this little old lady who lived along on a mountain in a log cabin that had a gigantic rock behind her house and it saved her life, the waters went right around the rock and around the house. She had only recently had electricity installed. She had never been outside Nelson County. Had never been to the White House, had never been to Washington. (less than one-hundred-fifty miles.) She used to walk I don't know how many miles to school as a kid. It was a fascinating story."

Miss Dora's neighbors had chipped in to have a telephone installed for her and Johnny gave her a call and talked to her on the air, taking Ken Ringle's advice that Dora was a proud woman. "He said she does not want pity." His listeners heard him talk to Miss Dora. "She was funny. I told her I read about her in the Post. She said she didn't read that paper. I said I would like to come down a visit with her. She said come on down."

Miss Dora did not have an easy life, or a modern one. Her neighbors cut her firewood, planted and cared for her garden and fixed up her place. She had no interest in the outside world, had never voted, didn't pay attention to politics, and was determined to remain in her ramshackle cabin until the end, even refusing to evacuate when floods took away her neighbors.

Johnny's on-air phone call produced an outpouring of help. "Food, clothing, all kinds of gifts for her. The American Red Cross helped."

Johnny kept his word to visit her. He took his young daughter Tracie along for the experience. He arranged for a pilot to fly them and the donated supplies by small plane to Lovingston for an afternoon. They flew out of Hyde Field in Clinton, Maryland, outside Washington. They were met by the Red Cross in Lovingston and drove by truck up to Miss Dora's place in the mountains.

"We pulled up in the truck and the dogs are barking and she's standing on the front porch wearing an apron, a little knit hat on, a stick in her hand. She was about five feet tall. She yelled at one of the dogs to stop barking."

His daughter Tracy asked to use the bathroom and Miss Dora took the girl around to the back to an outhouse, which Tracy had never used.

"I said we have some things we'd like to give you. We went inside. She opened the door to a room that was filled with boxes and gifts. She said, 'I don't know why people do this. I don't need this.' All of a sudden, something runs across the room. She said, 'Don't worry about that, that's old Freddy, he's a skunk.'"

His mission accomplished, Johnny, Tracie and the Red Cross volunteers left Miss Dora's and returned to the air-field for the flight home. "It was dark by then. When we were landing at Hyde Field the pilot realized he couldn't get down because the winds were so strong. He tried to pull it up and take it around one more time and as he pulled up it lost power and a wing hit the runways. The plane went up and it just nosed down."

The crash destroyed the plane. "Dave Statter (a reporter) from channel nine was on duty as a volunteer with the Prince George's County Fire and Rescue and got us out of there before the plane caught fire."

Statter was working as a disc jockey at a small radio station in La Plata, Maryland at the time but he was a volunteer firefighter in Prince Georges County on his off hours. "The call comes out just for a plane crash, doesn't say what kind of plane. It came out on Steed Road, which we know runs right by Hyde Field. In that area it could have been any-thing. It could have been a plane from Andrews (Air Force Base), it could have been a jet. We didn't know what it was. As we came down Steed Road we could see fire in the sky, you could see the glow of fire coming up, we could see smoke. It turned out totally unrelated. On that windy day there was a brush fire across from where the crash occurred. Most of the fire department units went toward the brush fire thinking it was the plane crash. It had nothing to do with it. A young woman in an ambulance calls in and says we've got the plane crash on the roadway on the other side of the airport. We went to help her.

"I remember it (the plane) was kind of nose down and the ambulance and an engine company were surrounding the plane. We helped them carry the victims out of the ambulance. I was helping carry the gurneys. I remember one of the people had a pretty banged up face."

The banged up face belonged to Johnny Holliday. Statter, a young broadcaster, knew who Johnny was but didn't recognize him. "I didn't know it was Johnny. Nobody mentioned that's Johnny Holliday. It was only later when we heard it on the radio."

Fire and rescue crews took the victims away. Says Johnny, "Then I went to the hospital and got out thirty days later."

It wasn't quite that simple. He, Tracy and the pilot were taken to Southeast Community Hospital where he was diagnosed with a broken nose and told to have his family doctor set it the next day. Tracy had some minor wounds. Part of his nose was behind his left ear. "How I could have gone home, I have no idea."

He called his wife, Mary Clare, who called their personal physician who ordered Johnny to go to Sibley Hospital immediately. The doctor there asked to see the x-rays. Southeast Community Hospital had not taken X-rays. The doctor at Sibley was appalled. Johnny's nose was set and tests were run.

"The next morning the doctor told me I had a ruptured spleen and there had been liver and pancreas damage." He was in the hospital for a month. If he had gone home after the crash he would have died.

Then, in 2003, Johnny went in for routine laparoscopic double hernia surgery. Following the procedure he had a reaction to the medication. “I came home and told Mary Clare my stomach was really hot. It was distended. I go the emergency room. I was hemorrhaging internally from a medication that should not have been given. I was in the ICU for ten days and in the hospital for about three weeks.”

While he was in the hospital he had a profound experience. “I can’t explain it. I dreamt that I could see a battle going on, clear as a bell. It was a gun battle. There were hooded horsemen riding up to this stone wall and motioning to me. I couldn’t see their faces, motioning for me to come on, come on. They would laugh and ride off. Then all of a sudden I could recognize their faces. The faces were all people whose funerals I sang at. Jerry Smith (a Redskins player), Wes Moore (a radio colleague), Bob Taylor, the guy in the mailroom at WWDC. All of these people were dressed in flowing gowns and hoods saying come on, come on, and the horses would rear up and they would take off again, gunfire going on and a battle raging.”

Johnny woke up and saw that his parish priest, Monsignor John Renzer, was sitting with him. “He said you were probably fighting to go or fighting to stay. He said, ‘It’s not your time.’ That was so real and it scared the living daylights out of me. The priest said, ‘Now you’ve been given another chance. Take advantage of it and do something good.’ And that’s why I think I wasn’t ready to die. If I was, I had two chances right there. I’m two for two.”

Some men see such events in their lives and wonder why a just God would put them through it. Johnny sees it as a message. “That’s why I feel there’s something up there watching over me. That’s why I feel guilty sometimes that I’m not living the life that I should. There’s always something else I can do. Now I try to live my life the right way to make up for some of my shortcomings.”

I've known Johnny for over forty-five years. I don't know what he means by shortcomings.

Part Fourteen

Cancer

Have you ever just sat and thought. Damn! I've been through a lot of shit?
Kermit the Frog (on Pinterest)

Sixty-three

I couldn't believe it.
Tom Glenn

There are some things we just don't like to think about, especially as we reach what marketers refer to as our senior years. Senior years is the first on that list. Another is cancer. Older people typically die of either heart disease or cancer. Most people would pick heart disease and its quick end, if they had a choice. Unfortunately, they don't.

A British study revealed that three-quarters of Britain's cancer deaths occur in people over sixty-five and half of those were people over seventy-five. More than half of all prostate cancer cases in the United States are in men over sixty-five. Grady Smith was diagnosed with prostate cancer and attributes it to Agent Orange from his Vietnam days, something he calls "a surtax for serving." He is cancer-free now.

Cancer is all around us. It is hard to find anyone who hasn't lost a family member or friend to cancer. My father died of it. My mother died of heart disease. She's considered the lucky one. Cancer has taken loved ones close to the men in this book. Jim King lost his daughter and his wife.

Two men in this book were diagnosed with cancer during the year I interviewed them, Tom Glenn and Jared Grantham.

"I should have been diagnosed in 2013," recalls Tom. "I had all the symptoms. I was even coughing up blood. But my primary care physician didn't call it, he didn't see it, he didn't send me for tests. He didn't think it was important. At the beginning of 2015 I was spitting up blood and I thought there's no point in going to the doctor because he says there was nothing to worry about. It started in February. I didn't go to him until May. He said maybe we should order an x-ray and they found a tumor. He ordered a CT scan and they found it again. He then sent me to an oncologist to immediately diagnose it." It was advanced lung cancer.

Within a week he was undergoing radiation treatment. That was followed by chemotherapy, which was followed by surgery to remove the tumor.

What was going through your mind when you heard the diagnosis?

"I couldn't believe it. For weeks I kept saying to myself, 'I have lung cancer!' and I thought that just cannot be. I just couldn't believe it. I knew it was true but my mind just couldn't accept it. It was a big tumor. It had been growing for some time."

His treatment made him miserable. "I felt terrible. I looked bad. But I got through it pretty easily."

During this dark period he lay in bed at night and considered the unthinkable.

"It was a death warrant. If you get lung cancer you die. I thought, this may be it. This may be the end of my life. I thought, what if it is true? What if I'm going to die? What will I do between now and death? I began thinking about all the things I wanted to do for my children. My will is all written. I had to worry about getting the house fixed up so it can be sold without a lot of trouble for my children. All those thoughts were going through my mind.

"The bigger issue was thinking to myself, this is death. I don't know what to think. I don't know how to face this. In my view, this is the end, there is no afterlife. There was a very cold feeling in the pit of my stomach. How do I come to terms with it in my own mind?"

This darkness, this profound question of life and death, was very different from his days in Vietnam when he believed he would not survive battles, when men standing next to him died as he fought beside them. Death, then, was not subject to profound reflection. "It was a matter of fact acceptance, the times when I thought I might get killed and I thought, well, if it is, that will be that."

Surgery happened fast. "I remember being sedated. All I remember is being there one minute and the next minute I was waking up from the surgery. Those first few days after the surgery I was very sick."

Earlier in the book Johnny Holliday described a near-death experience in a hospital bed. Tom also experienced a profound moment.

"I was conscious but I knew that death was right there and I could reach out and touch it if I wanted to. I could embrace it and if I did I would die."

What do you mean by that? What was it like?

"In my mind it was as though I was lying by a stream, very close to a black stream. And I could reach out and put my hand into the stream if I wanted to. I knew the stream was death. If I put my hand into it or if I rolled into it I would die. I chose not to do that. I didn't want to do anything like that. This went on for a long time, it was not as though it was a momentary apparition. I was not unconscious when this was going on. That's about as close as I can get in describing what it's like."

Did you consider living versus dying?

"I never considered living versus dying. The choice was offered to me and I said no thank you."

Now the cancer is in remission and he's looking ahead at whatever time he has left. "It seems to me it falls into two categories. One is to do as much as I can to make things easier for my children. That means selling this house and getting myself a townhouse somewhere and getting rid of my stuff. I have too much stuff. If I were to die while I'm living there (in a townhouse) that would be so much easier for my children."

Tom is, at heart, a writer. He's a very good writer. "The other things I want to achieve are all writing kinds of things. I have a book I'm ready to start sending out. I have two more I want to write. I'm not ready to go yet. I've got work to do."

Sixty-four

This is like a crucible.
Jared Grantham

During the year that I interviewed the men in this book two of them were diagnosed with cancer. The first was Tom Glenn. The second was Jared Grantham, who has faced serious health issues since the age of fourteen. He was diagnosed with liver cancer only weeks before his eightieth birthday. Any diagnosis of cancer is devastating. It is a bomb that blows up one's life. For Jared, a research physician, it began with a pain in his abdomen that intensified throughout the day. Carol, his wife, persuaded him to go to the emergency room.

"The pain that took me in stopped about two days after I went in and hasn't come back. It if wasn't for that pain, had I not caved and gone to the hospital that night, I would still be happy as a lark and not know anything was wrong with me. So, unfortunately, I found out a little earlier than I would have otherwise that I've got this pretty sizeable problem."

Jared is not a typical cancer patient. His body functions at thirty-per cent of what a normal man his age would experience. His body is disabled by polio that has taken a toll for decades. A few years ago he fell and broke his neck, nearly dying before he was revived. That, too, weakened him. Treatments that would be appropriate for other men will not benefit Jared and might even harm him. His treatment options are limited.

"The approach to it is palliation. It's not a cure. There is no way to cure this stuff. I will be starting chemotherapy. Palliation means trying to keep you comfortable. You can't cure it but you can maybe slow it down a little bit. There's a price to pay with that. I'm going to feel like shit. It's a matter of playing the potential of extending your life by six months or a year as opposed to investing maybe a few weeks or a couple of months feeling like crap to gain that extra time. I've agreed to do it up to a point. If I get to feeling too crappy, if the quality of life craps out, then I'm not going continue and let nature take its course."

Chemotherapy is a treatment that makes cancer patients' lives worse, not better. Jared's involves two drugs. Side effects could include colon perforations, small blood vessel issues, loss of appetite, loss of hair, and hands that turn red and peel. Not a welcome treatment for someone whose health is fragile.

"This is like a crucible," he says. "If you're lucky and don't have a huge collection of side effects you can sneak by and get a little benefit from the therapy."

Put yourself in Jared's mind. This is a man who has overcome obstacles that would grind most men into the dirt. He has always stood up, no matter how awful the experience, no matter how devastating the news. What is he thinking as he ponders his cancer and all that it means?

"I think maybe I'm psychotic. I'm not upset. I have not shed a tear since this all began. I'm locked in my own little world. I have enough things that I want to accomplish that I can compartmentalize this problem. When I start having more pain or other side effects, that may change because I won't have the mental firepower to keep me from thinking about my problems. That's a technique I've used all my life since I started having the 'shaping experiences' that I wrote about in my book. (*Why I Think About Urine.*) And it's the only way I've been able to survive breaking my neck, polio, the loss of Joel, my parents' deaths and all of that. I have the capacity to shift over to a different part of my brain."

Given all that he's been through, all that life has thrown at him, does he ever ask 'Why me?'

"I gave that up long ago. That's why I'm an agnostic. If God was really looking out for me why has he put so much shit on my shoulders? I gave up on that why me thing. It's all statistical. I'm just unlucky in that respect."

One week into his chemotherapy Jared was in low spirits. "In the last few days I've been getting to enjoy some of the side effects of this therapy. I have sores in my mouth. My heels are so sore I can hardly walk. That's part of the therapy. I've developed severe itching. I made the damn mistake of going out and sitting on the deck with my back to the sun for about an hour and a half, talking with my neighbor about my book. The sun was on the back of my neck. I didn't realize my neck was getting cooked. They told me, they said, 'Jared, this medication has a photo sensitivity aspect and you need to stay out of the sun and use a sunblock.' So the back of my neck and shoulder look like a lobster and it itches like crazy. It's just awful."

Itching, he says, is "really unnerving." He's had Carol and his home aides rubbing salves and ointments on it, but, "The last several days are as close to miserable as I've ever been."

His lifeline, he maintains, is his ability to separate his mind from his body, to compartmentalize, and work as a scientist at his computer. Carol went out to get a wheelchair for him to get around because of the pain in his heels, pain caused by the chemo.

He's losing weight. "I'm down to about 168 pounds." He lost five pounds in his first week on chemo. "My appetite is not as good as it used to be." There are several causes of the weight loss cancer patients experience. Mouth sores make it uncomfortable to eat. The cancer itself consumes energy. “I don’t know what goes on in patients who have metastatic tumors but I think the tumor eats more than the rest of the body does. It uses up some of the extra calories. You end up with something called cachexia, a wasting of malignancies, so I’ve got some features of that.”

As a physician Jared knows more about what is happening in his body than most patients enduring cancer treatment. “I’ve started cropping out these things called spider angiomas. I’ve got them all over my chest and my back and one on the tip of my nose. You see these in people who have alcoholic cirrhosis or in pregnant ladies. They are little blood vessels that pop up. They are kind of pretty to watch, little vascular abnormalities. Those are all things telling me that I’m not winning this battle, that’s for sure.”

When we talked he was not sure he wanted to continue with the chemotherapy. “I’m going to have to see some more encouragement somewhere than what I’ve seen so far.”

He has begun to get his personal affairs in order. “I’ve been spending a lot of time getting my books in order, instructions on how to handle the finances and that stuff, wills and trusts, and how to get into the stocks. I’m not sure I’ve got everything else organized that I wanted to.”

So that’s it, that’s where he is at this moment, one week away from his eightieth birthday. A man who sees himself at the end. Anyone looking at him from the outside would be astounded at his accomplishments. He’s travelled from a tiny high plains town where he carried chamber pots out in the morning to a scientist of world renown. He’s known pain and heartache that would break most men, but he’s always stood tall and moved on. And now he’s offering an example of grace.

"What I'm trying to do is make sure I make peace with everybody I know on this planet before that time comes. That I praise everybody I need to praise and thank everybody I need to thank. And be the best husband I can be to Carol as long as I can, and father to my children. That's heaven on Earth as far as I'm concerned. That's the heaven, right now, here and now, today."

We all ask ourselves, in our darker moments, what we would think and how we would handle it, if we could handle it at all. Jared has come to peace with it.

"I know the odds against me are extremely high. I'm ready to go. I really am. I've been fighting, as you know. I've spent a lot of time in hospitals, a lot of time feeling crappy. I'm just kind of worn out. At eighty years of age, given all the strikes against me, that's not bad. I've had a good run. I can't complain. Nobody is immortal."

A small pause, a reflection on the moment. "I just hope it can be something that is reasonably pain free. If not pain free, at least something that's comfortable and I can go without a lot of sound and fury. (pause) A nice myocardial infarction would be appreciated. (laugh)"

Final Thoughts and Lessons

Maybe all one can do is hope to end up with the right regrets.
Arthur Miller

There you have it. Seven lives. What to make of what these men have shared with us? Over the course of a year or so they have shared with me more than most of us would be comfortable telling a stranger. You, the reader, are the stranger they have just met. I hope they have become your friends. I hope they have inspired you to examine your own life. I sincerely hope they have inspired you to ask questions of the older people in your life. My parents died twenty-six years ago at this writing and there are still days when I wish I could ask them a question about their lives. What was it like growing up back then? What do you regret? What have you learned? How did you maneuver through the minefield that life can present?

I am staggered at the candor of these seven men. I was moved to tears by their losses. I was sent into personal reflection by their thoughts about religion and God. I was impressed by the solid values they live by.

There is a story several decades old now, perhaps apocryphal, about a young German man who sent a letter to the German Minister of Health, asking what he needed to do to live a good life. The reply was not what to eat or get plenty of exercise. It was to do the right thing by other people. By that definition, all seven of these men have lived good lives.

Jared Grantham is an example of a man who was flogged time and again by the forces that send men into decline, and yet, again and again, he got up, and achieved amazing things in his personal and professional life, earning the love and respect of everyone who knows him.

Tom Glenn's childhood was a nightmare by any standard. He was told he was too stupid to learn, his parents left him to raise himself, his older sister died of polio, and yet he set out to define himself and reach higher than those around him. This stupid boy speaks seven languages and has a PhD, had a distinguished career in intelligence and now writes books.

Grady Smith, the lad who left the seminary because he could not imagine a celibate life, who has the soul of an artist, was a career soldier with a distinguished combat record. He left the Army, got a PhD, and gave himself to the arts and to teaching.

Johnny Holliday, another boy with a terrible childhood, was unable to go to college because the money wasn't there. He got a job at a small Georgia radio station, found his place in the universe, and became one of the most beloved broadcasters in the business. He has a fine family, is a grandfather, and raises money for charities that help kids.

Jim Bohannon, a small-town Missouri boy who grew up among tree-lined streets and friends he knew as toddlers, went to war, came back, and used his big voice and big personality to host a nationwide radio talk show heard by millions every night. He's still amazed at his success.

Jim King, the boy who couldn't read until a teacher took an interest in him, became a cop, solved one of the biggest crime sprees in the nation's history, retired, and now writes books. His story of the loss of his little girl and his wife will bring a lump in anyone's throat and send you to hug your spouse and your children.

Lamont Gibson, who grew up on the mean streets of Cleveland and suffered through brutal and heartless racism, spent his life seeking fairness in the federal government, insuring that skin color, religion, gender or other differences cannot be used to deprive people of their rights and dignity. He is a man who can truly say he made a difference.

Listen closely to these stories. The times may be different but the basic question remains: How to live a good life? Not one of these men came from a privileged background and yet all of them were successful. Not one of them sees himself as a victim. Not one of them thinks the world owes him anything.

What's the secret to their success? It's very simple. Know what opportunity looks like, take it, and work your ass off. Do more, do better, work harder, and show up every day. Be kind. Be generous. Have high personal standards. Admit mistakes. Be grateful for what you have.

Sound familiar? It probably came from your mom or dad or your minister or teacher or some children's book. And they got it from the previous generation, and down through the ages. The quotes from wise people sprinkled through the book tell us that these basic life issues go as far back as humanity itself.

But right now, as you put down this book, resolve to find an old man sitting on a park bench, sit down next to him, and say, "Hey, Mister, what's your story?" You might be surprised at what he tells you.

Acknowledgements

Writing, we're told, is a lonely endeavor. It may be but it can't be done alone, at least not a book such as this. I must first thank the seven men who have shared their lives with us. Every one of them has a story worth telling. I also want to thank the men and women who took time to read this book as it came together, offering comments and insights. I want to offer my deepest gratitude to Karen Leggett Abouraya for first reading the unfinished product and then editing it to make it readable. She's been a friend over thirty years, a colleague, and a literate treasure. Larry Matthews

Gaithersburg, Maryland

2016

Meet our Author

Larry Matthews is a Peabody Award-winning broadcast journalist who lives and writes at his home near Washington, D.C. His thirty-plus years as a reporter provide the background material for many of his books, including the Dave Haggard thrillers ***Butterfly Knife, Brass Knuckles*** and ***Detonator***, hailed as "outstanding works of fiction" by reviewers.

His novel ***Take A Rifle From A Dead Man*** was recommended as a "must read" by the VVA Veteran, the magazine of the Vietnam Veterans of America.

Age In Good Time is Matthews' tenth book.

35863836R00160

Made in the USA
Middletown, DE
18 October 2016